Long Stays in the UK

Long Stays in
the UK

A COMPLETE, PRACTICAL GUIDE TO
LIVING AND WORKING IN THE UK

PETER McGREGOR EADIE

HIPPOCRENE
BOOKS, INC.

DAVID & CHARLES
Newton Abbot   London

HIPPOCRENE BOOKS
New York

Whilst every attempt has been made to ensure that
all information and prices are correct at the time of
going to press, the author and publishers can accept
no responsibility for any errors or omissions.

British Library Cataloguing in Publication Data

McGregor Eadie, Peter
   Long stays in the UK.
   1. Great Britain – visitors guides
   I. Title
   914.104858

   ISBN 0–7153–9376–6

Front cover photograph by Paul Mellor

Printed in Great Britain
by Billing and Son Worcester
for David & Charles plc
Brunel House Newton Abbot Devon

Published in the United States of America
by Hippocrene Books Inc
171 Madison Avenue
New York NY10016

Contents

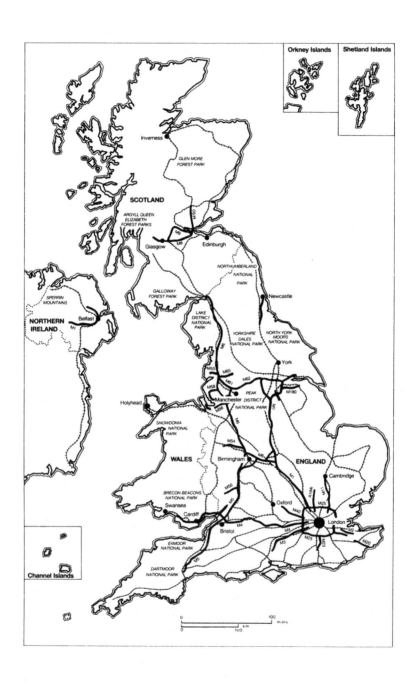

Orkney Islands

Shetland Islands

Inverness

GLEN MORE
FOREST PARK

SCOTLAND

ARGYLL QUEEN
ELIZABETH
FOREST PARKS

M90

M9
Glasgow M8 Edinburgh

NORTHUMBERLAND
NATIONAL
PARK

GALLOWAY
FOREST PARK

Newcastle

SPERRIN
MOUNTAINS

LAKE
DISTRICT
NATIONAL
PARK

NORTHERN
IRELAND

Belfast
M1

M6

YORKSHIRE
DALES
NATIONAL PARK

NORTH YORK
MOORS
NATIONAL PARK

M55

M65

York

M58

M61

M62

Holyhead

M56

M57

Manchester

PEAK
DISTRICT
NATIONAL PARK

M180

M1

SNOWDONIA
NATIONAL
PARK

M54

M6

Cambridge

WALES

Birmingham

ENGLAND

M1

BRECON BEACONS
NATIONAL PARK

M50

A1(M)

M11

Swansea

M5

Oxford

M40

M25

Cardiff

M4

Bristol

M4

London

M2

EXMOOR
NATIONAL PARK

M3

M25

M23

M20

M5

DARTMOOR
NATIONAL PARK

Channel Islands

100 miles
0
km
0 100

Introduction

This book is aimed at helping those people who wish to stay in the UK for varying periods of time, from several months to several years. People come to the United Kingdom of Great Britain and Northern Ireland for all sorts of different purposes. Some come on extended holiday; others are transferred here for company reasons; others are young people here to learn English and live in a family as *au pairs*, or to follow a course of study at one of our universities or other institutions of higher education. It is the hope of the author that visitors in all of these categories will find this book useful and informative both before and during their time in the UK.

The aim is twofold: to give the reader an insight into the character of the British people and their long history; and to offer practical guidance on preparation and settling in. Many useful tips are given on leaving your own country and arriving here, how to transfer money and chattels if required, and what documents are necessary on arrival for those intending to seek employment or to study here. The longer you intend to stay, the more you need to know about how to find accommodation, either to rent or to buy; the regulations with regard to both options are discussed. If you are planning to bring the family, you will find full information on the private and public education options available for different age groups, and an outline of the costs involved and how to find out about the scholarships and grants which are available to young people. Children with special needs are also catered for in the chapter on education. Those seeking employment or running their own business are given an overview of the different forms of taxation, as well as being directed to where more detailed help can be obtained. The visitor will find advice on how to open a bank account, raise an overdraft or secure a loan. In cases of difficulty, knowledge of the law and how to seek legal aid is also provided. Once here, you will also need to find out about doctors, dentists and hospitals, and a full chapter is devoted to health insurance, how to register for the National Health Service, and other important medical matters.

Anyone staying in the UK will want to see as much of the towns and countryside as time allows and several chapters deal with the different forms of transport by air, rail, road and waterways, and the various discounts that are available, as well as where to go and what to see. Much information is also given on events in different regions throughout the year, with particular emphasis on the arts – theatres, operas, concerts, ballets and festivals. Once again, addresses are provided in order to direct people to sources of greater information on sights and activities.

If this book helps to make your stay more enjoyable and trouble-free then it will have succeeded in its aim.

We must point out that the information given is based on data available at the time of going to press and nowadays rules and regulations, as well as costs, can change very quickly. So in certain matters, particularly to do with finance, taxation and even education, it is advisable, before taking action, to check details with the various authorities mentioned in the book.

The author is also well aware of the difficulty of avoiding errors, and suggestions for the correction and improvement of the guide will always be gratefully welcomed.

1
History and Background of the United Kingdom

The history of the early people of Great Britain lies buried in the strata of geological time, when Palaeolithic man disappeared following an Ice Age, along with his favourite dishes, the woolly mammoth and woolly rhinoceros.

When warmth returned to the soil, people generically referred to as Iberians came to inhabit the Mediterranean, the Atlantic seaboard and the British Isles. It is believed by some archaeologists that they built Stonehenge and similar structures, like Tarxien in Malta and Ggantija in Gozo. The accuracy with which the stones have been laid and the overall symmetry of Stonehenge, which is orientated towards the point where the sun rises on mid-summer's day, indicate a considerable knowledge of astronomy, combined with great engineering skills. It is not the work of primitive people but of a civilisation considerably advanced in many spheres of knowledge. Some of the heavy stones have been transported from a distance of about 200 miles. Stonehenge is a site that reflects a series of earthen monuments and stone structures erected over a long period of history. It was obviously a ceremonial centre that originally dated back to before 3000BC and was in use until at least 1000BC.

The arrival of waves of Celts during the sixth, fifth and fourth centuries BC supplanted the Iberians. Two main groups of Celtic invaders are distinguished by historians: the Gaels, who gave their language to the Scottish Highlands and Ireland, and the Bretons whose tongue became that of the Welsh. Although Greek and Roman writers refer to the Celts as a tall, fair-haired race, they did not all conform to the description and in fact, to hold this image, many bleached their hair. Some also dyed their bodies, and hence it was that the Romans referred to the Scottish Celts as Picts, derived from their word *Picti*, meaning painted men. These tribes had a liking for colour and today

9

many people believe that Scottish clan tartans originated with these Celts.

Having conquered Gaul, Julius Caesar crossed the Channel and, in 55BC, attacked England, but he met with fierce charioteers and was repelled. The following year the Romans returned. This time, having observed the enemy tactics and the terrain, Caesar brought his cavalry and won. Nearly a century later, in AD43, Claudius sent four legions totalling 50,000 men to Britain in order to establish a full-scale conquest.

However, the Romans could not defeat the Picts, and the Roman leader Hadrian had to build a fortified wall across the North of England in order to stop them raiding territory the Romans had already conquered. Today visitors to England will find place-names ending in 'chester' or 'cester' (from *castra*, the Latin name for camp) which indicates that these places, for example Colchester and Gloucester, were at one time Roman camps.

When the Romans left in order to shore up their crumbling empire elsewhere, the Anglo-Saxons and Jutes seized the opportunity to invade Britain. The natural harbours on the east coast made easy landfalls.

The Anglo-Saxons, who were basically of German origin, were tall and fair, fond of strong liquor, and an open-air people not given to living in towns. Their descendants are numerous, especially in East Anglia and Kent. They moved west, settling in the river valleys and lowlands until they were stopped by the Welsh tribes, who lived in more mountainous terrain. The Anglo-Saxons built villages and tilled the arable land in rotation, leaving one in every three fields fallow for each third year in order to avoid exhausting the soil.

The fifth and seventh centuries AD were a period of migration, and many of the Anglo-Saxon place-names that we find in Britain arose from the personal names of the people who came to live here. Others are settlement names. For instance the word end 'ham' denotes the word homestead or estate, and we find places called Caversham, Horsham, Heysham, Nottingham and Sandringham. Another example is the ending 'tun' or 'ton', used to indicate a farmstead or village. Hence such names as Carlton, Everton, Nuneaton, Skipton and Sutton.

During the eighth century the Norwegian Vikings, who

were later to travel as far north and west as Greenland and America, established themselves in the Orkneys. From there they colonised the Hebrides and the north of Scotland.

In the ninth century, drawn by the wealth of the Celtic monasteries, they plundered their way southwards, establishing trading posts from which some modern Irish ports have developed. The Vikings in Ireland were finally defeated by the Celt, Brian Boru, High King of Ireland, at the Battle of Clontarf in 1014.

From Ireland and the Isle of Man, Norwegian Vikings invaded England, and here they were opposed by Danish Vikings. One of the Danish Vikings, Sven Forkbeard, father of King Canute, declared himself King of England, also in the year 1014. King Harold finally defeated the Vikings at Stamford just three days before the Norman invasion began at Hastings.

Although not much archaeological evidence remains of Viking influence in England, it is well worth visiting the Jorvik Centre Viking museum at York. There an entire Viking settlement has been recreated, simulating the smells which emanated thence – quite an assault on twentieth-century noses. Today, their areas of settlement are deduced mainly from place-names. The most important monuments the Vikings left behind are runes, their script, which appear carved on stones, graves, ship burials and exquisite jewellery.

In 1066 William of Normandy landed in England at Hastings, where he defeated King Harold, who was slain by an arrow through the eye. This date is the most famous in English history. There has never been another successful invasion since, which is part of the reason why so much of Britain's historical heritage remains intact.

The Normans were descended from the same race as the Danish Vikings, whom Harold had just defeated at Stamford. This branch had acquired the Duchy of Normandy a century previously, but had then diverged so widely that the Danish Vikings in England were calling the Danes in France, Frenchmen.

William the Conqueror, as he was now dubbed, installed his followers in strategically placed castles and imposed a strong centralised government and efficient system of law. The conquest of England by the Normans linked her kingdom, commerce and culture to that of France, and, although there were certain benefits, the link also resulted in continued dispute over the control of French estates and territory. This, in turn, delayed the unification of Britain as the early Kings of England fought ultimately futile wars against the French. One of the battles in these wars, the battle of Agincourt, has been immortalised by William Shakespeare in his play, *Henry V.*

By the time Henry VIII came to power in the early 1500s, England was only a minor state on the north-western rim of Europe. The charismatic character of the Tudors was soon to change the scene. During Henry's reign ties were broken with the church of Rome and it was replaced by a state-controlled church. During Elizabeth I's reign, a strong navy under able navigators was created, and attention now turned away from Europe to the building of an overseas empire.

During most of the seventeenth century, under the reigns of the Stuarts, a struggle ensued about whether the sovereignty should lie with the Crown or Parliament. This led to a bloody Civil War in the mid-1600s and finally to a bloodless revolution near the end of the century. This was the last major political revolution in Britain. It saw the end of the divine rule of kings and its replacement by a parliamentary democracy and the triumph of common law.

In Britain the next two centuries saw the growth of naval supremacy on the high seas, and the development of a powerful free-trade empire.

At home came the birth of the Industrial Revolution, whereby technological development accelerated world progress into a new era. The latter brought with it grave social problems as greedy industrial barons extracted maximum work for minimum pay, which created appalling industrial slums. Conditions were aggravated by a population explosion as people were herded together in towns and cities. The inequities were half-heartedly tackled by nineteenth-century governments, and fiercely attacked by philanthropic organisations and great writers such as Charles Dickens. It was, however, not until the twentieth century that the British government can be said to have addressed the problems with a feeling of responsibility for the welfare of the people.

The first half of the twentieth century saw two major wars

in which this country, along with others in Europe, faced an enormous death toll among her young men. On the western front in the trench warfare of 1914–18, the average life of a subaltern was three weeks. The financial cost of these wars led to the demise of Britain's empire and industrial leadership.

There were, however, certain positive cultural benefits from these wars, in that attitudes changed regarding human rights. This led to a transformation of the empire into a Commonwealth of independent nations, and the slow growth of harmony between the different nations in Europe, which continues to develop and has recently received a boost with the liberation of so much of eastern Europe. The formation of the European Community (EC), of which Britain is an important member, plays a dominant role in this growth towards greater harmony.

The welding together of the four countries of England, Scotland, Wales and Northern Ireland to form a United Kingdom (UK) is the result of an evolutionary process of historical, economic, constitutional and social development over several centuries. The outcome is a rather unusual political system, combining monarchy and parliamentary democracy.

The Governmental System

The three main constituents of Parliament are the House of Commons, the House of Lords and the Crown. Although the monarch, currently Queen Elizabeth II, is the personification of the State in the UK and is the head of the three branches of government – the executive, the legislature and the judiciary – the role now confers little political power. Over the centuries the personal power of the monarch has been reduced and passed to ministers, who make most of the executive decisions. For example, the speech the Queen gives at the opening of Parliament is prepared for her and outlines the government's programme for legislation. However, the Queen's signature is required on all legislation and, although this is only a formality, it would be wrong to consider that the Queen, who is deeply respected and loved by her subjects, is not without a certain emotional influence.

The House of Commons exercises the political power. An elected government is voted in an regular intervals by the people, and is led by the prime minister and the Cabinet.

No government can exceed a period of five years without a general election. At each election 650 salaried members of the House of Commons are voted in, and each member represents a constituency or particular geographical area. The main political parties to be elected for over the past half-a-century have been either the Tories or Conservatives, or the Labour Party, although there are several other important parties which have gained sufficient votes for some of their members to be elected to the House.

The leader of the party who commands the majority of votes at a general election is invited by the sovereign to form the government, and he or she becomes prime minister and forms his or her own Cabinet. The party which obtains the second largest number of votes becomes the official opposition party, with its own leader and Shadow Cabinet.

The principal organ of the executive branch of government is the Cabinet, which is responsible for the implementation of laws. Ministers are collectively and individually responsible for all action taken by their departments. They answer to Parliament on these matters and this constitutes the most important democratic control by Parliament over the executive.

The main function of the legislature is to make laws regulating the life of the country and, in so doing, make available the necessary finance. Legislation on subjects other than finance or representation, which must be introduced by the Commons, can be initiated in either the House of Commons or the House of Lords.

Procedure is as follows. After its first reading, a Bill's general provisions are introduced and debated at a second reading. The Bill is then discussed in detail for amendments by a committee, after which it is reported to the House where further amendments may be made. After this it receives a third reading and, if passed, is sent to the other House for the same procedure. Then any amendments made by the Second House are reconsidered by the House originating the Bill. After all stages have been completed and agreed, the Bill is sent to the Queen for Royal Assent, which nowadays is a formality.

The judiciary branch of government, responsible for enforcing the law, is independent of both the executive and the legislature. It comes under the jurisdiction of the House of Lords, whose president is the Lord Chancellor. The Crown, acting on the advice of ministers, creates all judicial appointments. However, a judge of the superior courts can only be removed from office by the monarch at the behest of both Houses. There are different courts, and the highest court throughout the realm is the House of Lords.

Local government – the administration of public affairs in each locality by a body which represents the local community – has been part of the administrative system of the UK for centuries. In England and Wales administration of local affairs and services is handled by locally elected authorities. They include county councils, which are usually responsible for planning, roads and traffic, consumer protection, the police and fire services etc, and which share other duties and services with district councils. These include administering such things as housing, galleries, museums, libraries and parks, as well as social services, education and environmental health.

Administering and funding schools and institutions of higher education (other than private schools and universities) is usually the responsibility of local education authorities. They also administer the student grants given for courses at universities and other places of higher education, such as polytechnics. The financing of these services is mainly paid for by a new form of tax, referred to as the poll tax.

Local government is run along broadly similar lines in Scotland and Northern Ireland.

2
Modern Britain

The population of the British Isles is over 50 million, and England is one of the world's most crowded countries. Greater London, which covers an area of some 625sq miles, houses around seven million people. Almost 80 per cent of British citizens live in towns, and certain industrial and manufacturing areas, such as Greater London, Manchester–Salford, Birmingham–Black Country, and Leeds–Bradford, support half her urban population. In Scotland the narrow industrial belt between Edinburgh and Glasgow is home to four-fifths of her population. In Wales, Cardiff and Newport have the heaviest concentrations and, in Northern Ireland, Belfast. Although there is a heavy concentration of people in the UK there are many regional areas, particularly the Highlands of Scotland, which are thinly populated. Many of these places attract holidaymakers in the summer.

Religion
The main religion in the British Isles is Christianity, and the great variety of denominations is the result of repeated schisms in the church. In England, during the sixteenth-century reign of Henry VIII, a revolt against the supremacy of the Pope led to a break with Rome whereby the sovereign replaced the Pope as head of the church. However, the organisation continued to be administered by bishops as in the Roman church. This breakaway episcopal church, generally referred to as Anglican, is today the major church of England and Wales.

In Scotland the Reformation gave rise to a Presbyterian church which differs from the episcopal church in that each area is under the authority of a presbytery – a body composed of ministers and laymen referred to as elders.

Later schisms within the church of England gave rise to the non-conformist churches. In the seventeenth century the Puritan movement, aimed at simpler forms of worship, resulted in Baptist and Congregational churches and the Society of Friends, or Quakers. The eighteenth century saw evangelical revivals and the founding of the Methodist churches. In the nineteenth century smaller schisms produced fundamentalist sects which interpret the Bible literally, and the start of the Salvation Army.

The pattern of Christian worship in the UK shows that Episcopalians are dominant in England, Presbyterians in Scotland, and Calvinist Methodists in Wales. Northern Ireland is subject to a cross-section of religious influences. Those Irish with Scottish ancestry are most likely to be Presbyterian, those who arrived in Northern Ireland from the south are likely to be Roman Catholic, and those with English ancestry (who are in a minority) are likely to be Episcopalian.

Ethnic Groups

The nineteenth century saw the start of an increase in the number of Jews living in Britain and the twentieth century brought immigrants from many of the former British colonies, among them Indians and Pakistanis who introduced the eastern religions. Nowadays nearly all the major British cities have a synagogue and an Islamic, Buddhist, Hindu and Sikh centre. Freedom of worship is a legal right in Britain.

During the past few decades this influx of different races and peoples, who have migrated and become British citizens, has arisen for many reasons: some to escape political or religious persecution, others to find a better way of life. The indigenous population has achieved a good record and reputation for accommodating minority ethnic groups.

The biggest minority group comprises those descended from the Irish people who left their homeland in the nineteenth century to escape famine and poverty. The period of Nazi persecution in mainland Europe in the thirties led to an influx of refugees, many of them Jewish. After the 1939–45 war many West Indians and Asians came here to work and enjoy a better standard of living. Among the different people, besides those already mentioned, who have come to settle in the UK you will find Americans, Australians, Africans, Chinese and Vietnamese.

Many of the members of the ethnic minority groups prefer

to live close together, perhaps in order to keep their cultural traditions alive, and others prefer not to isolate themselves and to mix with other social groups. On the whole, relations between different races and creeds are very tolerant in the UK, although it would be wrong to say that racial prejudice does not exist. Where it does, it is usually the result of ignorance. The average citizen in the UK has a positive and welcoming attitude towards all members of the community regardless of their racial type or background, and people who come to the UK for a long stay will find it much more rewarding if they make friends and mix with all members of the community. In this way they will become more integrated into the British way of life.

Racial discrimination is against the law in Britain. In 1976 the Race Relations Act made such discrimination illegal in employment and education, in training and related matters, in housing, in advertising, and in the provision of facilities and services. This Act provides direct access to civil courts by complainants and, in the case of employment discrimination, to industrial tribunals.

As a result of the Act, the Commission for Racial Equality was set up to work towards harmony between people of different racial backgrounds, to promote equal opportunities and to investigate unlawful discrimination. The commission has issued a code of practice on employment and a draft code of practice on housing. It has become the principal source of advice for the public on all matters relating to the Race Relations Act, and in certain cases of breach will assist individuals who have serious complaints. Furthermore, the commission also supports the work of over a hundred community relations councils. These are autonomous voluntary bodies which have been set up in different areas, particularly where there are large numbers of people who pertain to an ethnic minority, in order to look after the interests of these minorities at local level.

Women in Society
Attitudes towards women vary a great deal in different parts of the world. Visitors will be aware of the equality of attitude towards women in the UK when they see that the nation's recent prime minister, as well as the monarch, are both female (1990). It is also important to realise that equality between the sexes

is a strong principle in British society. Women are entitled by law to equal pay and equal opportunity, that is equal to men, and where jobs are concerned it is illegal to discriminate on the grounds of sex. The Sex Discrimination Acts of 1975 and 1986 make discrimination between men and women unlawful in the same areas as the Race Relations Act. Remedial action on employment lies with industrial tribunals, and other related grievances can be taken before the county courts in England and Wales or the sheriff court in Scotland. Similar legislation on sex discrimination and equal pay exists in Northern Ireland, and there the Equal Opportunities Commission has the power to enforce the Sex Discrimination Acts and the Equal Pay Act.

In Britain if a woman leaves her job to have a child, her position must be left open for six months for her to return. This is referred to as maternity leave.

In the past two decades in particular, the role of women in British society has changed considerably, partly due to economic circumstances, in that the cost of living has risen to such a degree that in many cases a good standard of living now requires a double income, and partly due to the realisation that life is better for everyone if men and women are accepted as equal partners. Thus childcare is today much more accepted as something to be shared between both partners.

This change in the woman's role in society has led to greater social freedom and independence, enabling women to gather in public places such as cafés and bars which were, in the past, much more of a man's domain and where women had to be escorted in order to feel comfortable. It would therefore be a mistake for a man brought up in another country to consider that, in modern Britain, a woman or women on their own were necessarily seeking male company when enjoying a meal or a drink in a pub or a restaurant.

The Law
Laws in Britain provide great protection for the private individual, frequently much greater than in other countries. Among the many laws which protect the ordinary citizen from harassment are the Sexual and Racial Discrimination Acts. The Consumer Protection Acts and the Landlord and Tenant Acts

protect him or her from being taken advantage of financially.

Freedom of Speech
This is an ancient right which Parliament has long upheld and the visitor to Speaker's Corner in Hyde Park will soon be made aware of how often the most outrageous suggestions are tolerated. There was a case some years ago when a speaker was holding forth in strong words on the necessity of abolishing the monarchy. A worried foreign visitor reported this to the nearest policeman on duty, who after listening and observing the situation, called out to the other members of the audience that they would be welcome to form a queue and march on Buckingham Palace. There were no takers, and the foreign visitor continued to listen to the diatribe, now realising that the speaker was considered to be giving vent to personal opinion rather than inciting listeners to high treason.

From the many protest marches seen in the UK over the years, it is clear that the average British citizen's attitude is often similar to that of Voltaire, who said, 'I disapprove of what you say but I will defend to the death your right to say it.'

Legal Aid
If at any time legal advice is required, the individual can go to a solicitor for guidance and assistance. But, as most people realise, this can end up being very expensive. Hence the best way to obtain advice is to start with the Citizen's Advice Bureau (CAB) where for a nominal sum of money, around £5 ($US 9)*, you can get half an hour's advice, legal or otherwise. If your problem cannot be dealt with by the CAB the staff will put you in contact with a solicitor who will tell you whether you are entitled to Legal Aid.

With Legal Aid, a solicitor need not be expensive. Legal Aid means that the government can pay part of your solicitor's bill, or even all of it. So you may get legal help free or at a low cost. Over half the people on Legal Aid pay nothing for it, but they still get the full services of a solicitor.

---

* $US1 = approx £0.55 (autumn 1990)

The Legal Aid scheme may be able to help with problems to do with:

Prejudicial discrimination
Housing, mortgage arrears
Jobs
Social Security claims
Criminal cases
Accidents
Credit, consumer issues, debt payment
Family and children
Divorce and maintenance.

There are three kinds of Legal Aid – Legal Advice and Assistance, also known as the Green Form scheme, which covers any sort of help you need from a solicitor and may include representation in some courts under 'Assistance by Way of Representation'; Civil Legal Aid, which covers representation in civil cases; and Criminal Legal Aid, which covers representation in criminal cases.

To get Legal Aid your savings and income must be below certain limits. Your income and savings will be worked out by your solicitor if you apply for Legal Advice and Assistance, or by the Department of Health and Social Security (DHSS) if you apply for Civil Legal Aid.

If you are not sure whether you qualify for Legal Aid, you can always ask a solicitor for a £5 fixed-fee interview. This will give you up to half an hour's advice for £5 or less. Most solicitors who do Legal Aid work will give you a fixed-fee interview.

Legal Aid for Criminal Offences
If you have been charged with, or received a summons for, a criminal offence, you have the right to apply for Legal Aid. It covers the cost of employing a solicitor to help you with your case and, if your case is heard in the Crown Court, it will also cover the services of a barrister. Legal Aid will either help you pay for the case, or will cover the total expenses of the case, depending on what you can afford (based on your disposable income and your capital). If you are acquitted, it is likely that anything you have paid will be returned.

You should apply as soon as possible after you have been charged with, or received a summons for, a criminal offence. The earlier you apply, the more time your solicitor has to prepare your case. There is no limit to the number of applications you may make and you may apply at any time until your case is heard. If the offence is serious and you are held in custody, you have the opportunity to ask your solicitor about Legal Aid at the police station. If you do not get to see a solicitor before you go to court, most courts will have a duty solicitor who can advise you on the day. You will be entitled to Legal Aid if the court decides you need help to pay the costs of employing a solicitor to defend you.

You have to apply to the court which is hearing your case. To apply you must fill in an application form, and a form which asks for details of your money, which you can obtain from the court or from your solicitor. A solicitor will be able to help you to fill in the forms. You must help by telling the court why you think you need a solicitor.

If the court refuses you Legal Aid you may, in some cases, be able to make another application to a special committee, unless the court has refused because it thinks you do not need help to pay. The notice the court sends to you will tell you if you can make such an application. You may consult a solicitor under the Green Form scheme about whether to do so. You will be advised about applying again to the court.

For less serious offences *only*, the court can decide to give you Legal Aid. If the court refuses you can apply again, but only to the court. If you have not been given Legal Aid, you can ask for it again when you go to court.

If you think the court has made a mistake, or not taken something into consideration and so refused you Legal Aid in error, or is taking too much as your contribution, you can ask it to recalculate.

Legal Aid will be granted as soon as possible after your application, providing the court thinks you need it. The court will tell you then how much you should pay, if anything. If you do have to contribute towards the costs, you must pay either weekly or monthly instalments for six months. If you cannot afford to pay when the time comes, you must tell the court immediately. You can either post your payments to the court, or take them in person. You will be told the address by the court. Once Legal Aid has been granted, the court will ask you to pay the first instalment within a week of the grant.

Payments in capital are made in a different way. They are taken in one lump sum, at the same time that aid is granted to you, or as soon as possible afterwards. The court can say you have to pay before the Legal Aid is allowed to start.

If you decide to refuse Legal Aid, because you don't want to pay towards the cost of it, you must tell both the court and your solicitor at once. If you do not tell them, you may be asked to pay something anyway. And if you can afford to pay but refuse to do so, the court can stop your Legal Aid.

You can get more information from the Legal Aid Board, which has offices in most of the major cities in England and Wales. You should telephone or write rather than attend in person.

There are similar Legal Aid schemes in Scotland and Northern Ireland. If you want to know about Legal Aid in Scotland, write to: The Scottish Legal Aid Board, 44 Drumsheugh Gardens, Edinburgh EH3 7SW (Tel: 031-226 7061).

For Northern Ireland, write to: The Incorporated Law Society of Northern Ireland, Legal Aid Department, Bedford House, 16–22 Bedford Street, Belfast BT2 7FL (Tel: 0232 246441).

The Small Claims Court
In cases of litigation there is nowadays an alternative to paying out large sums of money for reasonably minor matters, and that is seeking reimbursement through the Small Claims Court. Here, provided the money involved does not exceed £500, you can present your own case.

The Police
Britain's forty-three police forces are divided up on a regional basis and each division is responsible for its own area. Unlike many countries there is no split in the force between traffic, civil and political police. The functions of the force cover everything from traffic control to crime prevention, protection of people and property, investigation of crime and the arrest of offenders.

Control over possible abuse of police powers is constantly under surveillance and the ordinary policeman does not carry a gun. If anybody is arrested, he or she is entitled to ask the police to notify one person, either a relative, friend or solicitor. Furthermore the police cannot hold anyone for more than a certain length of time without seeking justification for their action before a court.

In normal circumstances you will find the British police very polite and willing to assist the visitor. The bobby on the beat looks upon himself as a public servant, much more than his counterpart in some other countries who behaves as though he is merely a guardian of the law and tries to instil a certain element of fear through his general demeanour.

It would be wrong to say that the police never exceed their powers, but due to the very strict control exercised over police behaviour this probably occurs far less than anywhere else in the world. A great effort has been made and is being made to improve police relations with local communities where problems of misunderstanding are likely to arise. Members of ethnic minorities are encouraged to join the police force.

The police can also advise on social problems and will direct people in distress to the correct social agency.

The Samaritans
One of the leading agencies for people in personal or emotional difficulties, and who need someone to talk to in confidence, is The Samaritans. Its telephone number can be found in a local telephone directory or by phoning directory enquiries. The Samaritans offer a 24hr service. There is plenty of assistance in the UK from caring people, both in and out of the police force.

The British Temperament
The British as a race are inclined to be shy and are brought up to respect people's privacy. You have probably heard the phrase 'An Englishman's home is his castle', which reflects his own belief in the importance of privacy. He also respects others' desire for privacy. This pattern of behaviour has earned the British and particularly the English a reputation for being reserved and even snobbish. Actually this is not the case. It is more likely to be politeness and shyness which stops the British from making the first move. On the whole, although you are unlikely to find the British ebullient, you will find that they are

friendly and welcoming. Generally speaking a friendship with a Briton develops slowly but, once formed, is usually lifelong and firmly based.

The opening gambit between the British is nearly always some comment about the weather; although they are inclined to make out that their weather is worse than it really is, it is true that the UK is a fairly cold place for much of the year. This means that they are not a society which meets in open-air cafés, as in many other European countries. The meeting place for a chat is likely to be a pub or someone's home. In summer the venue may change, and they will have a drink in the garden of some village pub, or a picnic in the country.

One word of advice. It is usual in British society to be fairly punctual with appointments and it is considered rude and irritating to be late. If something prevents you keeping an appointment on time, it is customary to ring and let the person you are going to meet know that you have been delayed.

In this chapter we have spoken in fairly broad terms about the UK and although England, Scotland, Wales and Northern Ireland are part of an economic and political unit, it should be remembered that they each have their own distinct cultural identities. Many regional characteristics point to this fact. For instance, Scotland has its own educational system; and the Welsh, besides receiving English-language TV broadcasts, also have their own Welsh-language TV channel. You will also find differences in temperament between people who live in the north and south of England, as well as between the Cornishman and the Londoner, and between a Lowlander and a Highlander in Scotland. Although high-speed trains, motorways and air travel have given great cohesion to the UK, you will be sure to notice considerable changes of accent and dialect if you travel around the country.

In Britain's cosmopolitan cities you will hear a vast range of languages besides English being spoken by people who have made their homes here, or are here on business, on vacation or to follow a course of study.

3
Preparing To Go

If you are coming to Britain as a family for a long stay, then the factor which decides the success or failure of the venture seems to be the amount of planning and preparation which has been put in before the family actually arrives. Those whose families join them later, when doubts about accommodation and money have been resolved, are likely to have fewer problems.

Depending on how long you are going to be in Britain, you may consider it less disruptive and problematic to leave your children at home with relatives because, if the children are young, you will probably have to look after them yourselves as domestic help is hard to find and expensive. There are private day nurseries which take children under school age, but many have waiting lists and the cost may be as much as £35 per week for each child. An alternative is a child-minder, who looks after other people's children in her own home. The cost is from £25 to £35 per week. A list of registered child-minders is available from the Social Services Department of any local authority. Local authorities and a few colleges may also run day nurseries but this is not a useful option as their waiting lists are too long.

If the children are of school age (from five to sixteen years) and you will be in Britain for six months or longer, you should be able to find a school to take them, although the schools run by the local authority may not have vacancies. Remember that taking them to school and collecting them each day, and looking after them in the holidays, may be difficult if both parents are out simultaneously either working or studying. Under the law, children under sixteen are not allowed to be left alone in a house for any length of time, so an older child cannot be left to look after younger children.

Visas
As a visitor to the UK you will need to have a valid passport or other document satisfactorily establishing your

identity and nationality. You won't need a visa if you are a citizen of the Commonwealth (including Australia, Canada and New Zealand), but visitors from Sri Lanka, India, Bangladesh, Ghana and Nigeria require visas unless settled in the UK and returning within two years, or under special circumstances. Visitors from the Republic of South Africa and the United States of America don't need visas to enter the UK. Nationals of EC countries can use a National Identity Card instead of a passport.

How long a visitor can stay in the UK is at the discretion of the immigration officer at the port of entry, and at first permission can vary from a month to a year. The key factor in making this decision is mainly the ability of the visitor to prove that he or she can support him or herself, and not become a burden on the state.

It almost goes without saying that anyone who is leaving his own country to stay in another for a long period of time needs to plan the event with care.

If you own a property and are going to leave it for several months or longer, you must plan for someone, either a friend or neighbour or even a company which deals with such matters, to keep an eye on it. Another option is to let the property while you are away. Here again, experience has shown many people who have chosen such a course that it is best to select a friend or relative as tenant, ideally one who is likely to take care of your property as though it were his own. And it is only intelligent and fair that you put into storage anything fragile which is of sentimental or monetary value, so that it cannot be damaged and later cause embarrassment.

Luggage

Perhaps the next thing to consider, after having prepared to leave home, is the luggage or baggage which you intend to take. In the old days many of the more wealthy people did not give a great deal of consideration to either the amount or the weight. Film stars Douglas Fairbanks and Mary Pickford took some three hundred cases when they went to stay in Greece.

Nowadays most people travel by air where, unless you want to pay for excess baggage, which can be very costly, you are limited to one or two pieces of baggage. A rough guide to what the passenger is allowed to take in weight is 23kg in economy class, 30kg in business class and 40kg in first class. Some of these weight allowances have been altered to encompass the number of pieces of luggage. Again, as a rough guide this can be two pieces for first and business class, and one piece for economy class. In all cases it will be a condition that no piece of luggage exceeds 157.5cm (62in) in total dimensions (length + height + width). It is obviously advisable to telephone the airline with which you will be travelling to check exactly what your luggage allowance will be on both inbound and outbound journeys. Unless, of course, you can manage like Rick Berg, the author of *The Art and Adventure of Travelling Cheaply*, who managed a six-year sojourn with only a small rucksack. You are always allowed to take into the cabin one bag, small enough to go under your seat, and as this is not usually weighed you can put your more heavy pieces, such as the gold bullion bars, in it.

If you cannot avoid your baggage being overweight, it is advisable to weigh it in advance and find out from the airline how much it will cost.

Terrorism and hijacking have now made most airlines much stricter regarding security. They always wish to know if you packed your own suitcase and they also like to know if there are any radio components in your luggage. Hand luggage always goes through the x-ray machine. Most x-ray machines will not damage photographic film but if you are concerned about this, in most countries customs officials will allow you a hand examination.

Luggage for the hold is subject to spot checks. Therefore it is advisable to make sure that you don't pack silly items like a child's toy gun in your luggage. All airlines have a list of items you are not allowed to take on board an aircraft.

Most of the main termini at major airports in Britain and Europe involve long walks from the aircraft to immigration. It is therefore advisable to purchase a small trolley for lugging your hand baggage around if you are elderly or disabled. If you want to avoid porterage with your main luggage (which is now a minimum of £5 in UK airports), it is also worth having luggage that has its own wheels attached. Some of the strongest and best luggage available today is that produced by Samsonite, which has done a great deal of research on customers' requirements.

It is worth spending some time to find the luggage to suit your needs and tastes. In the domain of rucksacks and camera bags, Karrimor has few equals.

Customs Allowances

Many people like to bring a gift for those with whom they will be staying, and in most cases gifts can be purchased more cheaply when you are travelling because they are duty-free and also free of VAT. It may therefore be useful to know the quantity of duty-free gifts you are allowed to bring into the UK. No one under seventeen years is entitled to tobacco or drinks allowance.

The allowances include:

1 litre of spirits, or strong liqueurs over 22 per cent vol, obtained anywhere outside the EC, or duty- and tax-free within the EC (ie from a duty-free shop), or 1½ litres of goods obtained in the EC with duty and tax already paid.

2 litres of fortified or sparkling wines obtained anywhere outside the EC, or duty- and tax-free within the EC (ie from a duty-free shop), or 3 litres of goods obtained in the EC with duty and tax already paid.

2 litres of still table wine obtained anywhere outside the EC or duty- and tax-free within the EC (ie from a duty-free shop), or 5 litres of goods obtained in the EC with duty and tax already paid.

60cc/ml of perfume obtained anywhere outside the EC or duty- and tax-free within the EC (ie from a duty-free shop), or 90cc/ml obtained in the EC with duty and tax already paid.

250cc/ml of toilet water obtained anywhere outside the EC or duty- and tax-free within the EC (ie from a duty-free shop), or 90cc/ml obtained in the EC with duty and tax already paid.

You may also bring in a total £32 worth of gifts, souvenirs and other goods, but not more than 50 litres of beer and 25 mechanical lighters obtained anywhere outside the EC or duty and tax-free within the EC (ie from a duty-free shop), or £250 worth of goods obtained in the EC with duty and tax already paid, but with the same restrictions regarding beer and mechanical lighters.

You may bring in 200 cigarettes, or 100 cigarillos, or 50 cigars, or 250g of tobacco obtained anywhere outside the EC or duty- and tax-free within the EC (ie from a duty-free shop), or

300 cigarettes or 150 cigarillos, or 75 cigars, or 400g of tobacco obtained in the EC with duty and tax already paid.

If you do not exceed these amounts you can pass through the Green Channel, which states 'Nothing to Declare', after you have collected your cases. But be warned, this does not mean that you will not be subject to a spot check, and if you are found to exceed the limit you can expect, according to the amount, to have to pay duty; have the goods confiscated; or be fined, depending on the seriousness of the extra amount you have tried to bring in undeclared. Hence, if you have any doubts about the amount of 'duty-free' goods you are bringing in, go through the Red Channel and declare them. Observation has shown that you are less likely to be searched going through the Green Channel if you are dressed conservatively.

On no condition whatsoever should you try to bring prohibited drugs into Britain, even if they are only intended for your personal use. This is a serious offence which carries a severe jail sentence. If you are on medicinal drugs it is wise to carry with you your doctor's prescription, to prove that the drugs are authorised.

If you arrive by sea, the same sort of regulations exist. Visitors arriving with their car can obtain a red or green sticker which they put on the windscreen to inform customs officials whether or not they have anything to declare. By car you can bring in more or less whatever amount of luggage you like.

A ship's passenger will find that most lines are generous with the amount of luggage they allow on board. However, don't bring too much if you are continuing your journey by train, as British Rail limits second-class passengers to 50kg and first-class passengers to 70kg. And remember that paying porters to deal with weights which you cannot handle personally is expensive nowadays. Also it is not easy to find a porter any more, although some railway stations now provide a limited number of baggage trolleys. Excess baggage on British Rail costs £1.60 per extra 5kg.

At the same time as you book your tickets to come to Britain, you can usually take out insurance for yourself and your luggage. This is a sensible investment. At many airports you can even take out insurance after you have passed through immigration control, if you have forgotten to do so beforehand.

Heavy Removals

People who are coming to the UK for several years and intend to set up home should know that it is possible to ship their belongings from overseas. There are many companies which carry out this work and hence in certain territories it is possible to obtain competitive quotes. You should remember, however, that there is always a risk in getting other people to move your personal valuables, in that they can be broken and damaged by a bad removal company. Everyone who has moved house has probably experienced this at some stage in their career. So it can actually be more expensive to use the cheapest.

Personally I would select a company that is used to moving antiques, even if it is more expensive, for the simple reason that such firms take particular care in the way they handle removals. They cannot afford to do otherwise, because their reputation for care is why they are used frequently by auctioneers and antique furniture dealers.

Pickfords, the company which claims to be the world's largest removers and which has offices or agents in nearly all parts of the world, moves house furniture from Europe by van or truck. Although it is difficult to give precise costs, the company estimates that the price of moving the contents of an average three-bedroomed house is £2,500–£3,000. Equivalent contents are shipped from many parts of the world by using 6.1m (20ft) containers, and the cost from Australia is £3,500–£4,500; from Africa, where your belongings frequently have to go via the Cape, in the vicinity of £4,000; and from India, around £3,500. It is more expensive to ship furniture from the US, partly because it uses different equipment in the form of lift van containers; the cost from this region is usually between £5,500 and £6,500.

Several companies produce videos about moving worldwide, which lay out how the firms operate, starting with estimates and going on through packing – a service that most companies prefer to do themselves – to shipping.

If you really want to take the matter of moving seriously, some organisations will transfer cars, offices and factories.

31

Pickfords has moved and set up in the jungles of Africa a power station built in the west.

The Disabled Traveller
Disabled travellers to the UK will find that the journey is not as daunting as they might first think. Provided that you give advance warning to surface and air carriers, they will offer the necessary service to remove any problems in getting from one point to another. Also, people in Britain are very considerate in providing a helping hand for someone in difficulty.

Every airline has its own handling agent who will make the necessary arrangements when you arrive at the airport. The agent will provide a wheelchair and see you through customs and onto an aircraft. Disabled people are always the first on to the aircraft and usually the last off. In some cases special electric cars carry the elderly and disabled along the long corridors of the terminal, and there are always people to help you get onto the aircraft and into your seat. The booklet *Care in the Air* gives more information and can be obtained from the Airline Users' Committee, Space House, 43–59 Kingsway, London WC2B 6TL.

At the airport, specially equipped toilets are available which conform to the latest standards. They are marked with a sign displaying the wheelchair symbol.

British Rail (BR) has published a useful leaflet entitled *British Rail and the Disabled Traveller*. Again, BR provides considerable help but it needs to be given advance warning. BR staff will meet the traveller at the station entrance with a wheelchair, and use luggage lifts if necessary to get you to the right platform. On board the train the wheelchair can be positioned near a seat to which you can be transferred; alternatively, in some of the latest second-class coaches a table has been omitted near the entrance and next to the toilet so that a wheelchair can be put in its place. A warning should be issued here. The entrances to train toilets are too narrow to allow a wheelchair to pass through, and difficulties will also be encountered in getting to a restaurant car. However, drinks and refreshments can be brought to the passenger. By radio-paging ahead BR guarantees that a helper will be available at your station of disembarkation to help you to a car or taxi.

Regarding coach travel, the Expressline owned by National

Express have what is called a 'kneeling suspension' which makes access for the elderly and partially disabled considerably easier than on a normal coach.

Nowadays more and more hotels are offering special facilities for the disabled traveller, and to get more information on these and other matters it is worth writing to the Royal Association for Disability and Rehabilitation (RADAR) at 25 Mortimer Street, London W1N 8AB (tel: 071-637 5400). This registered charity helps disabled people by identifying the problems they encounter and then taking the necessary steps to reduce or eliminate those problems. It finds suitable accommodation and facilities for the disabled traveller and also publishes a guide entitled *Holidays for the Physically Handicapped*, which is up-dated every year, and a quarterly journal called *Contact*.

Travelling With Money
It is not wise to carry too much money on you, for fear of losing it or having it stolen. If you do have to carry a lot of cash, distribute it in different places so that if you lose your wallet or handbag you have not lost everything. Having a money belt which you can wear under garments is probably the safest way of carrying any big sums. There is no restriction on the amount of cash you can bring into Britain in terms of sterling notes, travellers' cheques, banker's drafts, letters of credit or foreign currency.

At Heathrow and Gatwick Airports there are 24hr banks where you can change money or cash cheques. Otherwise banking hours are limited, usually from 0930 to 1530 from Monday to Friday, with a few banks opening on Saturday mornings. Bureaux de Change are found in an enormous number of places, including airports, railway stations, London Underground (metro or subway) stations and in main streets. They are open longer hours but charge more money for changing currency.

Don't forget that you can also use credit cards such as American Express, Diners, Visa and Mastercard for paying a good many bills throughout most parts of the world. If your card is stolen you have about 24 hours to notify the credit card company before you are charged for bills run up on your account. Hence it is important to look regularly to see that you have not lost the cards and to carry on you the phone number of the office you must ring in case of loss.

Upon arrival in Britain, depending on where you are travelling to, you should probably carry around £60 on you for fares, meals and miscellaneous costs.

Climate and How To Cope

Somebody once said that other countries have climates and the British have weather, so the question now arises as to what sort of clothes you should bring to the UK. There is no easy answer, British weather is both a national joke and never-ending source of conversation; you will find that all British people open their conversations with an observation about the weather.

Generally speaking the winter runs from the beginning of November to the end of February, summer from 1 May to the end of October, and the months in between are spring and autumn. However, the climate varies quite noticeably between the north of Scotland and the south of England. The best sunshine records for the UK are found in Jersey, just off the coast of France, and in many places in the Highlands of Scotland it is possible to ski in winter. If you are going to live on the east coast of Britain be prepared for the winter east winds, which come from the Russian steppes across the North Sea and can be bitterly cold.

Temperatures in the winter usually require warm clothes for outside, which means a good overcoat, sheepskin or tweed jacket, or anorak, plus heavy sweaters. Having said that, for the past two years it has been too warm in the south of England for the author to wear his sheepskin jacket. Central heating is now common throughout nearly all offices and in many homes, therefore it is uncomfortable to wear a heavy suit indoors.

In summer, light clothes are required, although some people have said that this statement could be misleading to visitors from very warm climates. Central heating usually stops by 1 May in most public buildings and offices, and sometimes you can get caught and find yourself quite cold. Sometimes, too, summer days in the northern hemisphere can see a considerable fall in temperature. This is probably the reason why all news on TV finishes with the weather forecast. The weather in Britain can be summed up in one word – fickle!

One thing is for certain in the unpredictable British climate: you should always come armed with a raincoat, and preferably an umbrella and a very stout pair of shoes that will not let in the water. You will probably find it cheaper and wiser to buy your clothes when you arrive in the UK, particularly if coming from a warm climate. Another reason for buying your clothes in the UK is that you are more likely to follow the current trends if you see the type of clothes other people are wearing.

British Summer Time, which is 1hr ahead of Greenwich Mean time, is adopted between the end of March and the end of October.

Learning the Language

Whether your long stay in the UK is for a holiday, to follow a course of study, or to work, or indeed a combination of all three, it is most important to be as fluent in English as possible.

You will find that in the UK people are lazy about speaking other languages, unlike the continent of Europe where most people, particularly shopkeepers and waiters, make a definite effort to understand the visitor's own language.

Obviously for holidaying purposes it is not as vital to speak English as it is if you are going to be working in this country. Nevertheless, as English is one of the most widely spoken languages in the world, it is useful both socially and professionally. The most important precondition to ensure a successful stay is that you speak, write and understand English, unless you are coming to the UK specifically to learn English (advice on this is given in chapter 6).

You will need to speak English well enough to find your way round cities, public transport, shops, libraries and other places, and to hold conversations with people you meet. If you are coming to Britain to study for a diploma or degree, English is even more important in order to follow lectures and contribute to discussions during your studies. On some courses you will probably need quite a good commercial or even technical vocabulary as well as basic English, and lessons are provided to assist people in these matters. If you are not sufficiently fluent the results of your studies could be disappointing, because of your lack of ability in the language rather than your ability in your chosen subject.

You will find that most universities and colleges will not accept you unless you can prove that you have reached a certain standard in English. If you wish you can check on the standard of your English before leaving your own country. Go to your nearest British Council office where the staff will assess your fluency, by giving you a special English Language test, under the ELTS (English Language Testing Service). Most places of higher education in Britain will accept a score of six as evidence of an acceptable level of fluency for academic study.

If your family is coming to the UK with you, it is almost as important for your partner to speak good English as it is for you. It is a very isolating experience not to be able to carry on a conversation in the language of the country in which you are living. Ordinary day-to-day life will become a hassle rather than an enjoyable adventure, and making friends could be difficult if you can't communicate.

However, if your partner is not fluent there are courses in English available throughout the country, which include day and evening classes. You don't have to worry about young children because they always have a natural facility for picking up a new language just by listening.

Student Benefits

If you are a student, remember to bring your International Student Identity Card (ISIC) with you. It will enable you to buy many of the special tickets and cards which are described later in this book (see chapter 9). You will also be able to take advantage of the student discounts which are on offer at theatres and many other places of interest. A major plus in Britain is that most museums and art galleries are free, and many have on display some of the world's finest art and historic treasures.

You can obtain your ISIC card from student travel offices, often located in or near your own university or college, or by mail from NUS Services Ltd, Second Floor, Rigby House, 34 The Parade, Watford WD1 1LN (Tel: 0923 55300).

The cost of the card is £4.00. You will have to supply

proof that you are a student and one passport-size photograph of yourself.

The National Youth and Student Discount Scheme (NYSDS) card comes free with ISICs sold in the UK, and can be purchased by young non-students from NUS Services. You will then be able to get a discount of around 10 per cent on such items as clothes and records, as well as in nightclubs, discotheques, restaurants and hairdressers. The card can be used in 23,500 outlets in Britain. As this is a joint operation between Countdown, who supply discount cards to their customers, and the NYSDS, watch out for the Countdown sign which means the card is accepted there.

It is also worth getting the Youth International Educational Exchange (YIEE) card, introduced by the Federation of International Youth Travel Organisations (FIYTO). FIYTO is a worldwide association of organisations which specialise in youth travel. The card is most useful if you are going to be travelling to several countries and is available to all young people under twenty-six years of age. It entitles you to concessions on travel, accommodation, and sightseeing services, as well as other discounts. You can buy it from tour operators or travel agents who are members of FIYTO. In Britain it is available from Top Deck Travel, 131-133 Earl's Court Road, London SW5 9RH, or from Students Limited, 3 Harcourt Street, London W1H 1DS. For a list of agents where the card is available, write to FIYTO, 81 Islands Brygge, 2300 Copehagen S, Denmark.

Family

The wife and children of a *male student* have a right to join him in Britain as long as he proves that he can accommodate and maintain them, and the whole family intends to return home at the end of his studies. To date, however, the husband and children of a *female student* have no such automatic rights. It is more usual for the husband and children to be allowed into Britain only as visitors of the female student, not as her dependants. Visitor's status is usually for six months in the first instance, with the possibility of a maximum of twelve months. This means that visiting husbands and children of female students do not share her National Health Service status and would require private medical insurance.

Pets

It is not recommended that you bring your pet to Britain with you for a stay of less than a year, because animals have to spend six months in quarantine and birds thirty-five days. If you do decide to bring a pet, you must apply for an import licence at least six weeks in advance of travelling. It is obtained from The Ministry of Agriculture, Fisheries and Food, Hook Rise South, Tolworth, Surbiton, Surrey KT6 7NF.

The penalties for bring an animal or bird into the country without a licence are severe. The maximum penalty is an unlimited fine and/or up to one year in prison. This rule about pets entering the UK is always enforced, in order to keep rabies and Newcastle disease out of the country. Having the animal vaccinated against rabies makes no difference to the rule, and any animal or bird found to have been imported illegally will most likely be destroyed.

4
Budgeting, Banking, Finance and Taxation

The Cost of Living

Whatever the purpose of your long stay in the UK, whether it is to take up an overseas post, start a new branch office, study, or just have a long holiday, it is vital to work out how you are going to be situated financially. It is worth taking the trouble to learn exactly how much it is going to cost you to live in the area close to your work, which districts you can afford and which you can't, whether you can afford the style of living which you would like and, if not, where you are prepared to compromise.

The cost of living in Britain depends to a certain extent on area. For instance, generally speaking it is more expensive to live in the south than in the north, and in a town than in the country. Anyone who plays Monopoly, a game based on London property, will know that the cost of living also depends on district; for example, it is more expensive to live in Mayfair than in the Old Kent Road.

In order to give some sort of picture of the general cost of living, let us take the examples of an executive and his family living in a four-bedroomed house just outside London who will commute to work, and a student studying in a university town (see p46).

It will cost a person in middle management living in an area such as Reading, from where it takes approximately 50min to reach London, between £190,000 and £250,000 to purchase a house with four bedrooms, two bathrooms, two reception rooms, and a modern kitchen, with central heating, garden and garage.

The income of such a couple will be taxed at approximately 25 per cent unless they find themselves in an upper income bracket, where the rate will rise to 40 per cent. The level of taxable income at which a couple start paying the higher rate, depending on allowances, is approximately £21,000 at present.

This couple will spend around £20,000 net a year to live a moderate and normal life. To give some idea of how this breaks down, we will consider the essential costs.

The Poll Tax

The Community Charge or Poll Tax, which every adult has to pay, is around £475 per annum in this area. The charge is set by local councils to cover public services. So in the case of a couple you have to multiply by two and, if children aged over eighteen and who are working live with you, add another £475 for each of them – although, of course, payment will probably be their responsibility. The Poll Tax varies throughout the UK and in different areas is between roughly £250 and £500.

The Poll Tax means that when purchasing a house you no longer have to consider the rateable value of the property in your budgeting, as before. This is good news for those who can afford an expensive property and bad news for those who can't, for they are both taxed at the same rate. People on low incomes can receive government help with the Poll Tax. There has been a lot of controversy on this subject, and many demonstrations against the new Community Charge; it has reached the point where there is likely to be a review and changes made to the existing arrangements.

Your Mortgage

When purchasing a property it is worth remembering that if you take out a mortgage of up to £30,000 you can get considerable tax relief. Many people, when purchasing an expensive property, are therefore inclined to take out a mortgage for this amount. As a guide, at the time of going to press, even with this tax advantage the amount that has to be paid back is £350 per month for a 25- to 30-year mortgage at the existing interest rates. This is about one-fifth of the £20,000 annual expenditure mentioned earlier.

Heating, Lighting and Cooking

Electricity, which is mainly used for lighting, cooking and heating water, would cost approximately £250 per annum in a modern, well-insulated house. Bills are paid quarterly. This amount would be less if you cook by gas.

Gas, which is mainly got from the North Sea, is cheaper than oil or coal and therefore most homes are centrally heated by this fuel. An average annual bill for a four-bedroomed house in a mild winter will be around £350. Obviously, this will be more if there is a severe winter and if you are used to having the central heating very high for most of the day, with all the radiators on. On the other hand, heating will cost less if you have every window in the house double-glazed. When purchasing a house it is important therefore to consider the cost of heating the home, and to check on whether the roof is well-lagged and the windows are double-glazed. It is a plus to have gas central heating when purchasing a house, and a minus to have oil or coal, which are more expensive. Again, bills are charged quarterly.

Water: Rates and Drinking It
Water rates are paid twice yearly and will probably come to around £220 per annum, which is expensive because in recent years the quality of drinking water has seriously deteriorated. As a result the purchase of bottled drinking water in the UK has expanded beyond belief. The government recently privatised the different water boards throughout Britain and the public is now expecting an improvement in the quality of drinking water, and probably an increase in the rates. Not to exaggerate the situation, it should be said that by and large it is safe to consume water from the tap, although the quality and taste leave much to be desired in many areas.

British Telecom
The government also recently privatised the telephone system and most private telephones are run by a near-monopoly, British Telecom, which makes several million pounds profit every year. Telephoning in Britain, compared with the United States and most other countries, is expensive. If you are phoning from a call-box and making what is termed a long-distance call, which is not necessarily very far, say Aberdeen to Edinburgh, in the morning, you will find it difficult to feed the 10p coins in fast enough to carry out a normal conversation. Hence the successful sale of Phonecards, which enable you to purchase your calls in advance. These are green and silver, look like credit cards,

and can be bought in Post Offices and newsagents all over the country in values from £1 to £20.

It is very important indeed to have some idea of the cost of telephoning. Basically, calls are charged according to time bands and distance. The time bands are:

Peak rate, 09.00–13.00 Monday to Friday (which according to the phone book is when most people want to telephone);

Standard rate, 13.00–18.00 and 08.00–09.00 Monday to Friday, and

Cheap rate, 18.00–08.00 Monday to Friday and all day and all night at weekends.

Distance categories are as follows:

Local area rate or 'L' rate;

Up to 56.4km (35 miles) or 'a' rate, and

Over 56.4km (35 miles) or 'b' rate.

There is also a 'b1' rate which applies to some frequently used routes over 56.4km (35 miles).

Finally there are calls which are made to mobile telephones which people carry in the car or with them. This is referred to as 'm' rate.

Costs are worked out on the basis of units and each unit amounts to 5.06p. Below is a chart giving the *length of time for each unit according to the time of day and distance called*, and the cost of calling a mobile phone (just in case one of the children decides to ring Daddy on the way to work). And finally, beside each of these in brackets, is what an average 10 min call will cost.

Category	Morning		Afternoon		Evenings/wkends	
	Time per unit	Cost of 10min call	Time per unit	Cost of 10min call	Time per unit	Cost of 10 min call
'L'	60sec	51p	85sec	36p	240sec	13p
'a'	26.25sec	£1.15	35.1sec	87p	81.8sec	37p
'b'	18.6sec	£1.63	24.8sec	£1.22	38.8sec	78p
'b1'	23.25sec	£1.31	31sec	98p	51.5sec	59p
'm'	8sec	£3.80	8sec	£3.80	12sec	£2.53

Cost=5.06p per unit

This chart may not mean much until you consider it from an accumulative viewpoint. For instance, a half-hour long-distance chat each morning to an elderly relative would cost £1,221 per annum. Many British people find they have to forbid their children phone calls until the evening, and nowadays many firms ask employees not to ring in the morning unless it is essential. Also, because of the high cost, most firms now monitor the calls made by employees.

On top of the charges already mentioned you have to pay rent on your line of £78.80 (private), £127.68 (business) per annum, plus a rental on an ordinary telephone of £14 per annum. There is also a connection charge if you have a telephone installed of £148.65 (private) and £162.90 (business). You may think that the rent of an ordinary telephone per annum is the same charge as buying your own apparatus, and you would be right. The disadvantage of doing this is that, if something goes wrong with your own telephone, British Telecom engineers won't come out to look at it, so you have to take it back to the shop where you purchased it.

Of course if you find that it is not your own telephone which is at fault, but the line or exchange, you will then be able to ask the engineers to come and rectify the problem. However, the time it takes to sort out these kinds of difficulties makes it more practical to rent a telephone from British Telecom.

What you pay in telephone calls per annum is therefore very much up to the family – a garrulous teenager can cost the parent a lot of money in telephone bills, and it is important for everyone to be aware of costs. Excluding business use, most people in Britain do not telephone until after lunch and try to keep their calls to the evenings or weekends, despite the inconvenience. The telephone charges mentioned here were those in operation in autumn 1990.

Food and Drink
The next major item in the houschold budget is food. Naturally, this cost depends on a wide range of factors. For simplicity, the author has taken some of the prices in an average supermarket in a middle-class area of southern England, at the time of going to press. Obviously some items can be bought considerably cheaper in smaller shops; food is generally

cheaper in areas where housing is less expensive and earnings are lower – such as certain parts of north-east England, or some poorer districts of our main cities and perhaps in some rural areas.

Fruit and Vegetables (per lb, or 0.454kg)
Oranges 40p
Bananas 59p
Apples 52p
Grapes £1
Avocado pear £1.20
Large melon £2.25
Large cauliflower £1
Large bunch of celery 90p
Onions 56p
Potatoes 20p
Tomatoes 55p

Meat (per pound)
Steak £4.75–£8
Minced beef £1.20
Lamb chops (English) £4.35
Pork cutlets £2.60
Chicken £1.30

Fish (per lb)
Haddock £3.16
Cod £2.75
Shrimps (cooked and peeled) £5.75
Mussels £2.25
Rainbow trout £4.25
Dressed crab in shell £3.75
Lobster £5

Dairy Produce
Eggs (free range) £2.30 per dozen
Butter £1.20 per lb
English Cheddar cheese £2 per lb
Large loaf of bread 65p
Milk 30p per pint

Double cream £2.50 per pint (but can be purchased in small cartons)

Beverages
Coffee £3 per lb
Tea £2.80 per lb
Mineral water 42p per litre
Orange juice £1 per litre

Alcohol
Beer £1.10 per litre
Cider 95p per litre
White wine (Muscadet) £3.55
Red wine (Côtes du Rhone) £3.20
Champagne from £10 upwards
Gin £11 (0.75 litre)
Blended whisky £11 (0.75 litre)
Cognac (3-star) £13 (0.75 litre)

On average, without alcohol, the food for three meals a day for two people eating moderately costs around £90 a week at the present time. Obviously, not many people eat three meals at home every day. The cost of eating out varies. A pub sandwich and beer is around £2.50–£3.

Eating in the ubiquitous Italian and Chinese restaurants costs between £25 and £40 for two people, with a bottle of wine. Expensive gourmet restaurants cost from about £50 per head upwards. Many people nowadays who want to dine out, if they are without the benefit of an expense account, will go for an evening meal at a pub. Lots of pubs are now serving meals and, with a bottle of wine, the cost for two people is around £20–£24 inclusive. There are, however, other cheaper alternatives – wine bars, and bistros, hamburger joints, pizza houses, cafés which open in the evening, and unlicensed restaurants where you bring your own wine.

In the present financial climate the high cost of living usually makes it necessary for both partners to work outside the home if they wish to maintain a standard of living which is acceptable to them. This means, of course, that neither partner wants the effort of cooking in the evening. Marks and Spencer and some other large food chains have seen a gap in the market here, and now sell a wide range of gourmet meals that only require heating. English dishes include steak and kidney pie, beef with vegetables, poached salmon, and fish pies, as well as a full range of vegetarian dishes such as cauliflower cheese, vegetables en croûte, prepared salads and so on.

Dishes from other European countries include pizzas, ravioli, lasagne, cannelloni, tagliatelle and various paellas. If you like Chinese food you can choose from sweet and sour prawns, barbecued beef ribs, crisp prawn wontons, spring rolls and Chinese-style vegetables and Singapore-style chicken. There is also a full range of interesting dishes from India, including vegetable curry and chicken madras. It is possible to purchase a full range of different dishes for a month and to make up a meal of three courses that will satisfy most appetites.

Another development which has arisen from both partners having to work is that in nearly every district small food shops/general stores have sprung up which stay open until 2300hr and throughout weekends. They are nearly all owned and run by Asian families. These shops provide an excellent local service for busy workers, who know they can purchase food and household goods when it is convenient. They are also popular with elderly shoppers, who often are not able or do not wish to make the journey to a supermarket because they are buying in small quantities and prefer the more personal service they get in these shops.

It has been commonly thought that supermarkets are cheaper than local shops, and this is frequently the case compared with local shops that stay open late. But the increase in supermarket prices in certain areas is now making it often cheaper to buy at many of the smaller specialist shops, such as the local butcher, baker and greengrocer.

Living as a Student

A single student will need about £5,500 a year (1991 prices) to live – this includes rent, heat, lighting, food, daily fares, medical insurance and other day-to-day expenses. This is an average figure – the cost of living is obviously more expensive in London than in other parts of the country (see chapter 6, 'Accommodation').

The minimum basic cost of living for twelve months for a

student couple is in the region of £7,900. If you have children you should add a further £950 to £1,500 for each child. On top of these basic costs you may need to add a sum for warm clothing for yourself and your family. Visitors coming from hot climates will find the UK cold for much of the year and they may need to use heating more than those of us who are accustomed to northerly climes. At the cheaper end of the accommodation scale you can find there is no central heating and that you have to depend on coin-operated gas and electric fires for warmth. This can be expensive during the winter, as on a very cold night you could expect to put up to £2.50 in the meter. You would need to think in terms of approximately £12 per week in coins for the meter. Students should be aware that the amount of time you get from the meter is under the control of the landlord, not necessarily the supplier. Hence when seeking accommodation in what we call 'digs', if you can find somewhere with central heating, this can provide quite a saving.

You will also need to bear in mind an amount for leisure expenditure and, possibly, medical insurance (see chapter 8, p86).

If you are coming here to study you should find out from your college the exact amount of fees payable for your particular course. Most first degree courses take three years to complete. If you are a national of an EC country and have been living in the EC for three years before the course starts, you are likely only to be charged fees at home student rates. If you are an EC national applying for a first degree course and you have not already done a similar course elsewhere, then you may be eligible for reimbursement of your fees by the British government. The college will be able to help you with information about this.

Banking and Looking After Your Money

Before decimalisation of British money our coins were large and readily distinguishable. They also had good purchase value. Today changes in the world economy have altered much of this.

Britain's decimal currency is based on the £ sterling which is divided into 100 pence. Copper coins include 1p and 2p; silver coins include 5p, 10p and 50p. The pound coin is made of a gold-coloured alloy. New 5p coins have been introduced which are smaller than the original. When paying a taxi or other bills in bad light be aware that the old 5p and £1 coins are very similar in size, and that the same goes for the 10p and 50p pieces. Paper notes now exist for £5, £10, £20 and £50. There are no longer any £1 notes in England and Wales. This means that when travelling abroad the smallest sum of money you can change into another currency is £5. If you are a student on a tight budget this can be quite important to remember. Scotland, Northern Ireland, Jersey and Guernsey produce their own notes. Be aware that the Republic of Ireland's money is now foreign currency and the Irish 'punt' (the Irish word for 'pound') has considerably less value than the £1 sterling at the time of going to press. Some UK and Irish coins look very similar.

Banking Facilities
In the UK there are an enormous number of banking facilities to choose from, and here I list a reasonable selection. They are: Abbey National Building Society, Allied Irish Bank, Bank of Ireland, Bank of Scotland, Barclays Bank, Beneficial Bank, Clydesdale Bank, Co-operative Bank, Coutts Bank, Girobank, HFC Bank, Lloyds Bank, Midland Bank, National Westminster (NatWest) Bank, Nationwide Anglia Building Society, Royal Bank of Scotland, TSB (Trustee Savings Bank) and so on. Every bank offers its own range of incentives to persuade you to bank with it. Hence it is necessary for every long-stay UK visitor to shop around before deciding with which bank to open an account.

Students will find that nearly all the major banks offer them special facilities in the hope of getting their account and perhaps keeping it after they graduate. The incentives can include cash gifts, free traveller's cheques, free student coach cards, cheap student loans, an insurance package, a discount on books, and so on.

What is important first of all is to select the type of account (or accounts) which is most suitable to your circumstances. In the UK you will find a very wide range from which to choose, such as current accounts, deposit accounts, gold deposit and special premium accounts that pay high interest on large sums of money deposited.

A checklist of facilities you would be wise to consider before deciding where to place your account should include whether you get interest paid on credit balance, whether you can become reasonably overdrawn without transaction charges, whether there is access to a credit or debit card, and whether you are given a £100 cheque guarantee card, which is pretty essential nowadays when you have to pay large bills in places where credit cards are not accepted. You can also use a cheque guarantee card in almost any bank in the UK in order to obtain cash, and if you also get a Eurocheque card this can be used in the same manner to withdraw cash from most European banks. Major credit cards can now be used internationally. No one wishes to carry around large sums of money, so make sure you are properly equipped with the essential plastic cards. But use them carefully, it is easy to run into serious debt without realising that you have done so when you are not paying cash.

Consider also whether the bank will give you a friendly and efficient service, with full itemised statements on a regular basis. Other things that can matter are whether there is a branch close to home, or where you work or study and, if you travel, whether the bank has lots of cash machines or bank branches. In some cases it may even be important that your bank opens on Saturday, as they used to in the old days but in some cases do not any more. If the bank you choose has cash machines that are easily accessible from where you live or work, you need not worry about Saturday opening as the machines enable you to withdraw cash when the bank is closed and, of course, when it is crowded.

Transferring Money from Abroad
If you wish money to be sent to you from abroad, this can be done either by foreign draft, which is a cheque written out in sterling, or by a transfer of money into your bank account in the UK. In the latter case it would be necessary for you to supply the person sending you the money with the name of your UK bank, its address and the number of the account into which the sum is to be deposited. Alternatively, the money can be transferred to any bank, but in these circumstances the receiver would have to establish his identity by producing his passport.

Money in an overseas bank can also be transferred to a UK bank, provided there are no currency restrictions in existence. It is of course more simple to carry out this operation if you are using a bank in the UK that is also represented in your country. Similarly, if you wish to send money home, equivalent procedures exist in the UK for transferring money. There is a special leaflet which you can obtain from any Post Office explaining its services and the costs involved, which are fairly minimal.

Post Office Savings
The Post Office, which has some twenty thousand branches throughout Britain, has an Ordinary Account which provides a simple way of saving. You can start it with £5 and the maximum you can have in the account is £10,000. The interest rate is low, with the advantage that the first £70 of interest per annum is tax-free and does not have to be declared. You get a bank book which shows at a glance how much money you have on demand, and how much you have deposited and withdrawn from the account at any one time. Withdrawals of £50 can be made daily without having to send in your bank book for checking. If you have held the account in a chosen Post Office for six months, you can apply for the account to be renamed a Regular Customer Account. This will allow you to withdraw up to £250 daily without having to send in your account book.

The Post Office Investment Account has a similar style of book. The minimum deposit is £5 and the maximum £100,000. The interest rate is more in line with the existing bank rate and the advantage of this account is that tax is not deducted at source, as in most other bank and building society accounts. This makes it a good account to use if you are not a tax-payer. One month's notice is required before money can be taken out of the account. Information on both these savings accounts is available from any Post Office, or by ringing National Savings Public Enquiries (071-605 9461).

Other products in the National Savings range that could be of interest to people whose long stay may cover a few years include Capital Bonds, which have capital growth with a five-year guarantee with no tax taken off at source; Savings Certificates, which have tax-free returns guaranteed over five years with a choice of fixed interest or index-linking and extra interest; and Income Bonds which earn a regular monthly income for lump sum investments. Details of these offers, along with others not discussed such as Yearly Plan, government stocks and premium bonds are available in leaflets that can also be picked up at your local Post Office.

Investment in non-government stocks and shares is another means of earning money, but for this you are advised to seek the assistance and advice of a reliable stockbroker.

Borrowing Money

There is often a time when it is necessary to borrow money for some purpose or other. In Britain credit has become widely available, and as a result the problem of debt is growing. If you need to borrow it is advisable that you have some idea of where to go and also what kinds of loans to avoid.

For sensible borrowing, it is important to know the APR (Annual Percentage Rate) on your loan. It is worked out in the same way for every type of loan, and makes it easy to compare one with another and then calculate which is most suitable for your situation. Another matter to consider is whether the interest on your loan will vary with interest rates in general. With a variable rate the interest you have to pay can either rise or fall, but with a fixed interest rate you always pay the same amount of interest as was agreed at the time of the deal.

Credit Cards

Probably the most common way of acquiring a loan is through a credit card. There are quite a variety of these, of which the most popular are Barclaycard and Mastercard or Access, and it is possible to hold a number of cards. The companies who provide the cards set your credit limit, based on what you ask for and what they are prepared to offer.

You can use a credit card in a large number of shops, restaurants and other retail outlets, and for withdrawing money from certain cash machines, up to your set limit. The first twenty-five days of borrowing are interest-free but after that, at the end of the credit month, you either have to settle up the amount owing – in which case you have had a free loan for a short period – or you have to pay back a minimum monthly sum of either £5 or 5 per cent of the amount outstanding, whichever is the larger. It

51

should be remembered that cash withdrawals are charged from the day of withdrawal, and there is also a handling charge of 1.5 per cent for this facility.

The APR on credit cards ranges from around 19.5 per cent to 30 per cent and is variable. It should be mentioned that most of these cards, which until recently were provided free of charge, are now in a transitional phase and it is likely that soon there will be an annual fee for owning one. The fee will have to be paid to the supplier of the card.

Bank Overdrafts

For a short-term loan in times of difficulty, a negotiated overdraft facility on your bank or building society account is a useful accommodation. Overdrafts can usually be arranged with your bank manager up to an agreed amount according to your circumstances. APR on overdrafts varies and in some cases the overdraft can be free of interest and charges; also, if you are a student it is possible to obtain an interest-free facility. It always pays to discuss overdraft facilities with your bank manager, as authorised overdrafts nearly always incur a lower APR than unauthorised.

Ordinary Loans from a Bank or Building Society

Interest on the ordinary loan is nearly always variable, but can be fixed when the deal is struck with the bank manager. APR varies from around 17 per cent to 23.5 per cent. What normally happens with an ordinary loan is that the bank pays the sum into your current account and you pay it back into a separate loan account in regular, agreed sums. Many banks offer ordinary loans that are negotiable. They are often not advertised, but it is worth asking if your bank does offer ordinary loans because they can be a better buy than personal loans.

Personal Loans from a Bank or Building Society

These loans are not as inexpensive as ordinary loans (see above) but are probably more widely available and easier to organise. Upon borrowing a specified amount for a certain period, usually from three to seven years, you pay back a regular amount of the loan plus interest in agreed instalments. The APR ranges from 19.15 to 34.5 per cent and can be fixed or variable.

Other ways to Borrow Money
These include credit unions, employer loans, insurance policy loans, mortgages and equity release schemes on property, shop credit, and many others which may be worth considering according to your circumstances and requirements.
Loans through trading check companies, who provide vouchers which enable you to purchase at a network of retail and service outlets, are an expensive way to borrow. Their APR can be as much as 50 per cent. There are also disreputable moneylenders whose APR goes through the ceiling. Be aware of the APR on a loan before borrowing and use sensible loan facilities.

Child Benefit
This is social security benefit paid to anyone bringing up children. As it is fairly complicated it is only possible to give general guidance here. If you need fuller information, contact your local Social Security office. You will find the address in your telephone directory under 'Health and Social Security'. You can also write to The Child Benefit Centre, DHSS, PO Box 1, Newcastle upon Tyne NE88 1AA.

You can get child benefit for any child under sixteen or any child under nineteen who is studying full-time up to 'A' Level standard. You do not have to be the parent of the child to qualify. The child must be living with you or, if not, you must be paying at least as much as the child benefit every week towards the child's support.

It doesn't matter how much money you have or how much you *earn*, if you are entitled to British child benefit, your earnings won't affect it. However, if either husband or wife has any earnings which are exempt from UK income tax, then it will not be possible to claim child benefit.

Although you have only just arrived in Britain, you may be entitled to child benefit if you have come from another EC country to work for an employer in Great Britain. You may also be entitled to it if you have come from Australia, Austria, Belgium, Canada, Finland, Germany (Federal Republic), Gibraltar, Guernsey, Isle of Man, Jersey, New Zealand, Northern Ireland, Portugal, Spain, Switzerland or Yugoslavia.

If you are an **Australian** and intend to stay in Great Britain for less than three years, you will remain entitled to Australian child endowment for the period of your journey and for the first twelve months of your stay in this country – this is, provided that the journey takes less than thirteen weeks. After that, Australian child endowment will usually stop but by then you may be able to claim British child benefit. If your stay in Britain is to be for at least three years, residence in Australia will help you to get British child benefit.

You should claim any Australian child endowment owing to you immediately you arrive in this country from The Registrar, Department of Social Security, Australia House, The Strand, London WC28 4LA.

If you remain liable for Australian taxes, Australian child endowment is payable for the whole time you are away. You cannot claim both Australian and British child benefit for the same child at the same time.

You will receive **Austrian** family allowance if you work in Britain but you and your children normally live in Austria, or if you remain compulsorily insured under the Austrian social security scheme. If neither of these applies to you, but you have residence in Austria, it is worth applying for British child benefit.

If you are normally resident in **Belgium** but are not covered by the EC social security arrangements you should apply for British child benefit. If you are entitled to both countries' benefits, you can choose which one to receive. Where the benefits would be payable to different people, the authorities will decide.

Canada, New Zealand and Switzerland. If you are going to live for a substantial period in the UK, and are a national of any of the above countries, you will find that if you retain a residence in your own country this will greatly facilitate your efforts to obtain British child benefit.

If you are not covered by the EC arrangements and you are insured under the **Federal Republic of Germany (West Germany)** social security scheme, you will receive German family allowances and you will not get British child benefit. If not, your residence in the Federal Republic will help you to get benefit in Britain.

If you have come to work in Britain from **Finland** and remain insured under the Finnish scheme you will continue to receive Finnish children's and family allowances. If you do not remain insured in Finland, then the fact of your residency in Finland will help you to get child benefit in this country. Finnish allowances may be paid to a person who is responsible for any of your children in Finland. If you are entitled to benefit from both countries for the same child, benefit will only be paid by the country where the child lives.

If you are normally resident in **Mauritius**, this will help you to get British child benefit while you are in Britain. If you are entitled to benefit in both countries for the same child, then it will only be paid by the country where the child lives.

New Zealand benefits cannot normally be paid outside New Zealand but there are some exceptions for temporary absence. If you continue to be eligible for New Zealand benefit, you will probably find that it will be paid in arrears on your return to New Zealand.

If you are compulsorily insured under the social security system existing in **Portugal**, you will continue to receive Portuguese family allowances while in Britain and therefore will not be entitled to claim British child benefit. This is the case whether your children are in Portugal or in Britain. If you are not insured under the Portuguese scheme but have residence in Portugal, this will help you with your claim for child benefit in Britain. Portuguese benefit may be paid to a person responsible for any of your children in Portugal. If you are entitled to benefit in both countries, it will only be paid by the country in which the child lives.

Spain. If you have been sent by your Spanish employer to work in this country you will remain compulsorily insured under the Spanish scheme, and entitled to Spanish benefit. If you are entitled to benefit from both countries, benefit will only be paid by the country in which the child lives.

If you are insured under the **Yugoslav** social security scheme, you will receive Yugoslav family allowances and will not be entitled to British child benefit. If not, and you are employed in Britain, residence in Yugoslavia helps you to get British child benefit.

You may also be able to claim if you or your husband or wife has become employed or self-employed since entering Britain, and intends to stay for at least six months; and if you and your husband (or wife) received child benefit at any time within the past three years. Both you and the child must be in this country when you claim.

Taxation

Those coming to Britain for a long stay and who will be working either for a company or for themselves are likely to be liable to some form of British tax. The tax system is complex but the Inland Revenue, who administer Income Tax, Corporation Tax and Capital Gains Tax,and HM Customs and Excise, who control Value Added Tax, have many offices throughout Britain and are pleased to provide information. Both bodies publish a full range of explanatory leaflets free of charge, which give detailed guidance on all aspects of taxation. Addresses and telephone numbers can be found in the telephone directory.

Professional advice can be obtained from accountancy firms, who will charge for their services. Anyone working on a self-employed basis would be well advised to consult a qualified accountant.

Income Tax

This tax is assessed under six schedules which categorise the type of income being received; they are lettered form A to F and in some instances are sub-divided into 'cases'. Husband and wife are treated independently.

(a) A person employed by a UK registered company will be assessed under Schedule E. This system is known as Pay As You Earn (PAYE), and the onus for collecting the tax rests with the employer. PAYE only operates on income from employment; any other form of income (eg dividend) would be assessed under another schedule and collected direct by the Inland Revenue. Not all income is subject to tax. To enable the employer to charge the correct level of tax, the Inland Revenue issue all persons on PAYE with a Notice of Coding (often referred to as a tax code). Application for a tax code must be made by the individual to HM Inspector of Taxes at the local Inland Revenue office.

(b) *Self-employment.* Income from a trade or profession will normally be assessed under one of the cases in Schedule D. Normal practice is to take the trading profit of the business and then adjust it to arrive at a taxable profit.

Capital Gains Tax

The UK also has a *Capital Gains Tax* (CGT) whereby a taxpayer can make net gains of approximately £5,000 on his or her assets in any one year, before the rest is treated as the top slice of income and charged to CGT at income tax rates. There are certain assets which are exempt from this form of tax, such as the main home, ordinary private motor cars, British government stocks etc. A list of these is obtainable from the Inland Revenue.

VAT (Value Added Tax)

You may have heard of VAT. Many self-employed people complain about the amount of time it takes to keep abreast of the work VAT involves. VAT is based on turnover, and the present regulation, at the time of going to press, is that you must register for VAT if your sales are likely to be above £22,100. For more information on registering, make contact with Customs and Excise (whose telephone number will be in the local phone book) when you set up your business.

The present rate of VAT is 15 per cent. When you buy goods or services for your business, you are likely to be paying VAT on some of them. If you register for VAT, you may be able to claim back some of this tax. However, you will then have to add VAT to the cost of your own goods and services (unless they are zero-rated or exempt). This will increase your prices but not your income. If the amount of VAT you pay out exceeds the amount you collect, you are entitled to claim back the difference.

Corporation Tax

Companies pay corporation tax on their profits after the deduction of certain allowances, and all companies paying dividends to shareholders are required to make an advance payment of corporation tax to the Inland Revenue. The main rate of corporation tax for companies earning profits under £200,000 per annum is 25 per cent, with the main rate being 35 per cent on profits of £1 million or more. Marginal relief is allowed between the two figures of £200,000 and £1 million.

Setting Up a Business

Setting up a business on your own in the UK can be both confusing and daunting. It will be necessary for you to obtain considerable knowledge quite quickly, not only about your income tax but also about national insurance, VAT, corporation tax etc, and you will need to know which government department is responsible for which function.

To help you, an information pack is available which brings together advice on the main government regulations. This can be obtained by contacting the nearest Small Firms Centre or the Enterprise Agency in the area where you intend to start business, or by telephoning 071-273 4964/5. The pack, which is called 'Working for Yourself', is free and also gives information about where to obtain expert help on how to run your business.

The above information on income tax, VAT, capital gains tax and corporation tax applied at the time of going to press. It should not be taken as an accurate assessment of existing tax laws. It is essential to realise that the Chancellor of the Exchequer in the UK keeps all these matters under constant review and the latest information on certain specific taxes can quite quickly go out of date. Hence the author hopes that what has been written will be a useful guide to those visitors who come to the UK to seek employment or start up a business; but it must not be taken verbatim as the exact conditions existing at the present moment. For up-to-date information enquiries need to be made to the government department concerned with the above matters.

5
The World of Work

Reviewing the Situation

It is very important to be aware that, given the current economic climate in Europe, finding employment in the UK is extremely difficult. You should not travel to Britain intending to work unless you have already made arrangements for employment before you leave. Unless you have the correct documentation for your visit, you will be refused permission to enter the country.

EC nationals do not need a work permit (though in some cases permits are still in the process of being phased out). They may take any job with permission from the Department of Employment. However, generally speaking jobs are difficult to get and even EC nationals may not be able to find work. The unemployment situation in Northern Ireland will make the task of anyone looking for work there even more difficult. It is therefore unrealistic for a student to consider trying to work his or her way through college.

Work Permits – who needs them?

Commonwealth citizens and foreign nationals who are full-time students are permitted to work part-time or during their vacations in certain circumstances, as outlined later in this chapter.

Under UK immigration rules as they stand at present, certain categories of workers do not need work permits. These include doctors or dentists coming for postgraduate training in hospitals, ministers of religion, representatives of overseas newspapers, news agencies or broadcasting organisations, and employees of an overseas government. Also, professional sportsmen and sportswomen taking part in competitions of international standing do not normally require permits. If you are not sure about whether you need a work permit or not, contact a UK representative in your own country, for example at the British Embassy or British High Commission. Or in the

UK, you can go to any Jobcentre or contact the Department of Employment, Overseas Labour Section, Caxton House, London SW1H 9NF (Tel: 071-273 5336 or 071-273 5337).

You will need a permit to work in the UK if you are subject to immigration control and if you do not come into any of the categories mentioned above.

There are also some restrictions regarding age, which apply unless you are an entertainer by profession. An overseas worker should normally be aged between twenty-three and fifty-four years. However, if you are a sportsman or sportswoman the lower age limit does not apply.

Getting Your Work Permit

The application for your work permit will have to be made by your employer in the UK. He will have to complete form OW1, which he can get from his local Professional and Executive Recruitment (PER) office or Jobcentre. Their addresses are in the telephone directory under 'Manpower Services Commission'.

It is worth bearing in mind that a genuine vacancy must exist in the work for which you are applying, and that there must be no suitable labour available in the UK to fill the vacancy. The employer will have to make adequate efforts to fill the vacancy from resident labour or from other member states of the EC.

The application must be for a named worker to fill a specific post, and the pay and conditions of employment must be as good as those being offered in that part of the country for similar work. You will also be expected to have enough knowledge of the English language to do the job, and you will need to be able to show that you acquired your qualifications, skills and experience outside the UK.

What your Prospective Employer must do

Before your employer can get the go-ahead from the Department of Employment to offer you the job, there are several things he has to do. It is worthwhile being aware of these, and checking that you really fit the bill can save you a lot of wasted time.

The requirements are detailed in form OW1, but the main things the employer will have to do are as follows. He will have to consider carefully whether the vacancy can be filled by the promotion or transfer of an existing worker, perhaps after suitable training. He must let the PER office or the Jobcentre know that the vacancy exists, and allow four weeks for a suitable local worker to be found. He must advertise the vacancy in the local, national or EC newspapers, as well as in the appropriate professional and trade journals. He will have to be willing to pay travel expenses for any suitable applicant in the UK to come for an interview, or to take up employment. If he believes that it would be useless to look for a worker to fill the vacancy either in the UK or wider EC market, he will have to be able to convince the Department of Employment of this.

What You Can Do to Help
You can help your employer by supplying him with the right information, such as documentary evidence of your qualifications. If at all possible, your references should be original ones, not copies, and should be on headed business paper. Each one should be signed, dated and stamped with the employer's official stamp. They must show the type of employment and the exact date that each appointment started and ended.

It is very important to give yourself plenty of time to find work and get your permit, because your employer will need to apply for it at least eight weeks in advance.

If you are granted a work permit, the way it is sent to you depends on your nationality. If you are a Commonwealth citizen living in a Commonwealth country or Pakistan, the permit will be sent to you through the UK government offices in the Commonwealth country concerned. You will be notified when the permit is on its way to you. In the case of other nationalities, the work permit will be sent to the employer who will then send it on to you.

Professional Qualifications
Obviously you will find it easier to get a work permit if you have recognised professional qualifications. The following categories of worker are looked on with the most favour: administrative and executive staff, highly qualified technicians with specialised experience, and workers with a high or scarce

qualification in an industry or occupation requiring expert knowledge or skills. Permits may also be issued to highly skilled and experienced workers for senior posts in hotel and catering work. They should have completed successfully full-time training courses of at least two years' duration at approved schools abroad, or have other relevant specialised or uncommon skills and experience.

Sportsmen and sportswomen who meet the appropriate skills criteria, and established entertainers, including self-employed entertainers coming to the UK to fulfil their engagements, will normally be given a permit. There is also the fairly exceptional situation whereby the Secretary of State for Employment will grant a permit if he thinks that to employ a particular worker will be in the national interest.

Training and Work Experience
It is also possible to get a permit if you are coming to the UK for a limited period of training or work experience. You or your prospective employer should contact the Home Office, Immigration and Nationality Department, Lunar House, Wellesley Road, Croydon, Surrey CR9 2BY (Tel: 081-686 0688) for detailed information on this and other immigration matters.

If you have a Wife and Children
A dependant wife and/or children under eighteen years may come with the overseas worker, or may enter the UK later, but they will not normally be given entry clearance until you are in possession of a valid work permit. They will need to get entry clearance from the British Embassy, Consulate or High Commission in the country where you live. You will be asked to guarantee in writing that you will be able and willing to maintain them and to provide a home for them in the UK, without help from public funds.

Arriving in the UK
When you arrive in the UK the immigration authorities will want to see your work permit, a valid passport (not an identity card) and, if necessary, a visa. Without these documents, entry to the UK may be refused, but if all goes well you will be allowed to stay in the UK for the period specified in the work permit.

Changing Your Work

If your employer later wants you to do a different type of work for him, or to work for him at a different address, he will have to re-apply to the Department of Employment and complete form OW1.

If you or your employer want to end the employment you are both free to do this without the consent of the department. The work permit is not a contract of employment. It does not bind you and your employer together nor does it allow the employer to force you to stay if you wish to leave. However, you will need permission from the Department of Employment to change to another job, and the department will expect it to be the same type of work for which your work permit was issued. Notice of termination must have been given either by you or your employer. If your prospective employer can show that there is no suitable resident, or EC, labour available for the job you intend to move to, he should send an application on form OW1 to the Department of Employment, Overseas Labour Section at the address given earlier in this chapter. Otherwise the application on form OW1 should go to the local PER office or Jobcentre.

Staying On

If you are happy in your job and want to stay on in this country after your permit runs out, you – or your employer on your behalf – must make an application in writing to the Home Office two or three months before the work permit has expired. You will not need an official form, but you must enclose your passport and a police certificate of registration or, in the case of a Commonwealth citizen, either the employment certificate or Department of Employment letter of approval. You must also supply a letter from your employer stating how long he wishes to keep you in the job for which the work permit was granted.

Working Students

Students often want to take employment when they come to the UK, working either in their spare time or during the vacations, and they need the permission of the Department of Employment to do so. They also need to provide satisfactory written evidence from the place where they are studying that the work they want to do will not affect their studies. Permission will be given only if there is no suitable resident labour available for the job, and if the wages and other conditions are at least as good as those offered for similar work in the area. Again, the application should be made by the employer on form OW1 and sent to the PER office or Jobcentre.

Au Pair

Single girls, aged between seventeen and twenty-seven years inclusive with no dependants, who are nationals of a western European country, including Malta, Cyprus and Turkey, may come to Britain as an au pair, living as a member of an English-speaking family. The contract is that the au pair helps with household duties and with looking after children for a maximum period of five hours daily, and in return she is provided with free food and accommodation, a small amount of pocket-money, and enough free time to follow a course of study.

More information on au pair arrangements can be had from the British Embassy or Consulate or British Council office in the visitor's home country. On arrival in Britain it will be necessary to have a letter from the family with whom you will be staying, giving details of the family, the duties they would like you to carry out, and the pocket-money and time off you are to have.

Another matter to consider is homesickness. Parents should give careful consideration to their daughter's temperament before encouraging her to come to Britain as an au pair. The trip is supposed to be an enjoyable experience, and someone who pines for home will not make the most of it.

If a girl in her teens or early twenties wants to be an au pair, her parents should first of all make every effort to find out about the family with whom she will be staying. Try to find out if the family comes from the same standard of background as your child is used to, whether they are likely to be congenial, what sort of age the family's children are, and how they behave and so on. Parents should consider carefully whether their daughter is best suited to living in the country or in town, and here it pays to remember that public transport is expensive for someone who only gets pocket-money.

The best situation of all for someone sending their daughter to Britain as an au pair is, to know a friend whom she can go and see – preferably one who lives not too far away from the family with whom the girl will be living.

There are a number of au pair agencies in the UK who can help with finding positions. All official au pair agencies are required by law to be licensed, and come under the inspection of the Department of Employment. Agencies are not allowed to charge a fee for finding an au pair position, but are allowed to charge for other services, provided they first inform you in writing of what the charges will be.

The Federation of Recruitment and Employment Services, whose address is 10, Belgrave Square, London SW1, is a leading voluntary association for private employment agencies. This federation has a strict code of practice for its members and will send you a list of au pair agencies on request.

Several other reliable organisations give assistance in arranging au pair posts. Upon receipt of an international reply coupon they will give advice. The International Catholic Society for Girls, whose address is St Patrick's International Youth Centre, 24 Great Chapel Street, London W1V 3AF, provides such a service for posts throughout Britain and organises regular weekly get-togethers for au pair girls, where they can make friends. The society also runs a counselling service.

Most areas in Britain are safe for young girls to go out. Nevertheless it is advisable for au pairs to take advice from their local family about whether it is sensible to go to certain areas of some of the larger cities at night.

Already in the UK and Wanting to find Work

If you are already in the UK and you decide you would like to take a job, the rules are slightly different. The overseas visitor may not be allowed to work in this country if the original reason for coming here was other than employment; for instance, if he or she came here on holiday or to study. In such cases the Department of Employment will not consider an application for employment until the Home Office has decided whether the visitor's conditions of stay allow him to take employment or, if not, whether the conditions can be changed. The prospective employer will need to send the visitor's passport with the application and, if he or she has one, the police certificate of registration. Some non-Commonwealth nationals are required to register with the police, depending on the terms and length of their stay.

The British Workplace and What to Wear

Generally speaking, jobs or positions fall into a variety of categories. The executive is usually expected to wear a suit and leather shoes, and to look smart and businesslike. Suits are frequently worn by women executives, while office workers of the same gender can be more casual. The same standard is expected of many of the professional classes, such as doctors and lawyers. Those working in the more artistic fields, for example actors, authors, journalists, painters, designers and draughtsmen, are not so bound by convention. The very nature of their jobs often demands that they should dress with a certain amount of flair, in order to create an impression.

Blue-collar workers whose jobs are manual as well as mental usually dress in clothes which will stand up to harsh treatment. Among this group are included carpenters, steelworkers, Post Office workers, garage engineers, builders, factory workers and so on. They wear jeans, overalls, shirts, sweaters, anoraks, and heavy boots or trainers. They are not expected to look smart and don't have to follow the conventions of the executive group.

Some jobs demand that uniforms are worn. Such workers include aircraft personnel, members of Her Majesty's forces, chauffeurs, commissionaires, etc. In some cases uniforms are supplied with the job, in other cases they have to be purchased by the individual.

Fringe Benefits

The executive group often finds that the job carries a number of fringe benefits, such as a car, free medical insurance, luncheon vouchers and, often, many other types of assistance. These benefits are used to attract executives who expect to attain a certain high standard of living while also having to pay fairly high taxes. Executives also get good annual leave (from three to six weeks a year), although they do not always find the time to take it all. Nowadays the atmosphere in the workplace has become so demanding and competitive that some executives are at their desks by 7 or 8am and stay long after office hours to keep up with their workload.

The blue-collar group do not get the same fringe benefits, but usually they are not expected to work overtime. If they do work overtime they receive extra pay, which usually goes up to 1½ times the hourly rate. One of the major benefits that the blue-collar workers have is that the trade union, to which in many cases they have to belong, negotiates annual pay increases on their behalf.

Holiday Allowance
Compared with many countries, British annual holiday leave is generous. It ranges usually from a minimal annual period of two weeks, up to six weeks. The average is three or four weeks. Nowadays nearly everyone in the UK has a long break between Christmas and the New Year, which is an added bonus.

Of course school teachers and university lecturers get the best deal where leave is concerned, with considerable free time between terms. Even so, some of this vacation time has to be spent preparing for the coming academic year.

6
Accommodation

Temporary Accommodation
It is possible to arrange temporary accommodation before your arrival by writing at least six weeks in advance to the London Tourist Board and Convention Bureau, 26 Grosvenor Gardens, London SW1W 0DU. They will make a provisional booking on your behalf and will write to you about it. Once you have arrived in London you would do well to visit the Tourist Information Centre at Victoria Railway Station (open 09.00–19.00 Monday– Saturday and 09.00–17.00 on Sundays, with slightly longer hours in midsummer). They can arrange an hotel booking for you. There is a £4.00 booking fee and a £6.00 returnable deposit. There is also a Tourist Information Centre in the main concourse of the London Underground station at Heathrow, which is open 09.00–18.00 every day of the week. The British Tourist Authority office in your own country will also be able to help you in advance of your departure.

A wide range of hotel accommodation throughout Greater London can now be booked by telephone, using a new service just launched by the London Tourist Board (LTB). This booking service is on 071-824 8844 and is available to Mastercard and Visa card holders from Monday to Friday, from 09.00 to 18.00. Multi-lingual staff will be able to offer the caller accommodation at a range of prices. All the establishments on offer will have been inspected to meet the LTB's standards. Callers will pay a deposit of £10.50 (deducted from the final hotel bill) to secure their room, and a £4.50 booking fee, and will receive telephone or written confirmation of their booking. If you reserve hotel or permanent accommodation from a definite date but fail to arrive on time, you will lose your deposit.

Accommodation for Students
Most English language schools and organisations in Britain will arrange accommodation for their students. This is usually done

with a British host family, so that you will be able to practise your English outside the classroom and in an ordinary day-to-day environment. It also gives you the opportunity to learn something about British family life. Some English-teaching organisations offer a wider choice of accommodation, including residential, hostel and hotel accommodation. Some schools can even arrange rented flats for long-term students.

If you are coming to the UK to take up a scholarship, such as those administered by the British Council, you will be given help to find accommodation when you arrive. It is advisable to ask about living arrangements when you apply for your place in college.

If you are going to be studying at a polytechnic or college of further or higher education you will be able to get guidance from the college authorities. Every university in the UK has an accommodation officer who can give advice and help to private students, as many first-year students must be resident in approved accommodation. If you have not been able to make arrangements in advance of your arrival, be prepared for difficulties in finding furnished rented accommodation at a reasonable price because the demand greatly exceeds the supply, especially in the big cities and the university towns.

It is worth arriving early in the area where you are going to study, in order to give yourself time to look for suitable accommodation. While you are looking you may have to pay a fairly high rate for temporary accommodation.

Students in London
Full-time students studying in London will find that the British Council's Accommodation Unit is a very useful source of help for long-term accommodation. You should take documents confirming that you are following a particular course of study and details of your financial position. The British Council has offices throughout the UK, witih headquarters at 10 Spring Gardens, London SW1A 2BN (Tel: 071-930 8466).

Rented Accommodation provided by Universities
This ranges from residential colleges, halls of residence, and houses for small groups of single students, to flats for married

students. However, there is rarely enough accommodation to go round so again it is very important to apply to the university accommodation officer as soon as you are accepted on a course.

Polytechnics and Colleges of Higher and Further Education
Most have their own student hostels where you may find a place, but be sure to apply to the warden of the college as soon as you have been accepted.

Rented Accommodation in Hostels
This type of accommodation varies quite a bit in what it offers. Some hostels have rooms for either single or married students, and some provide food, while others are self-catering. Names and addresses of some of the hostels offering accommodation are available from the borough council of the area where you intend to stay. London, for obvious reasons, has the largest amount of hostel accommodation.

The Bedsitter
This means you have one room to live in and you share a bathroom. Sometimes there are very simple cooking facilities in the room, but you may have to share a kitchen.

Digs or Lodgings
This usually takes the form of a bed-sitter in a private house; you will, in effect, be sharing someone's home. You can expect to pay rent by the week, every two weeks, or monthly. What you pay will include breakfast or, in some cases, breakfast and evening meal (this is called half-board).

Married Students
Some accommodation for married students is provided by colleges and voluntary organisations, but it is often booked up in advance before the end of the previous academic year. As there is a shortage of housing everywhere in the UK you will find yourself competing for somewhere to live with many British families and groups of young people. Therefore it is most important to plan ahead and give yourself plenty of time to search, and to be prepared to be fairly flexible in your approach.

Renting a House or Flat
This is a rather expensive option unless your company is helping with relocation. Some companies in the UK have property which is made available to employees from abroad. If you are renting on the open market you will have to sign a lease, usually for a minimum of six months to one year. You will probably have to pay your rent monthly and there will be various rules regarding the property, which are legally binding. The lease will state, among other things, how much notice is required on either side to terminate the arrangement. The landlord's and tenant's rights are well protected by the law and if you need advice on any aspect of your agreement it is wise to get some guidance from the Citizens' Advice Bureau. You will find the address of your nearest branch in the local telephone directory.

In Britain there are letting agents in many of the cities and large towns, who take a 10 per cent commission of the total rent for up to a year's renting, which then reduces in following years to 7.5 per cent. Such letting agents have an association which can advise you about who offers a reliable service in your area. Equivalent organisations also exist in other countries, and people coming to the UK would be well advised to seek professional services if they intend a long stay. Again it must be emphasised that such a company needs to be conscientious and reliable. A leaking roof or burst waterpipe can be a horrendous experience if there is no one to see to it.

Buying a House
Most people in England and Wales use an estate agent to buy and sell their homes. In Scotland it is more common to use a solicitor's agent. Many estate agents are now part of a large chain linked to financial institutions.

Estate agents don't charge buyers, so it is advisable to sign on with as many agents as possible in the area where you are interested in living. It is also a good idea to look out for advertisements in the national and local papers. Many people try to sell their homes in this way. Don't accept everything you read in estate agents' particulars as being correct. They are not covered by the Trade Descriptions Act.

Most agents and solicitor's agents charge a commission to

the vendor based on a percentage of the selling price of the property, so their fees have rocketed in line with house prices. Fees are much higher in Greater London where properties are more expensive. Their charges also reflect the higher costs of running an estate agency in London. You must be prepared for the fact that buying a property can be quite a lengthy business, because it is a very large capital investment; usually you will be involved with someone who is himself in the process of selling a house, which results in an even lengthier operation.

It is always wise to get a surveyor to carry out a survey on a property you intend to buy, to see there is no dry rot or structural defects. To see that there are no plans to demolish your property, or to build a motorway outside your front door, it is best to employ a solicitor to carry out appropriate searches. The solicitor can also deal with drawing up the contract on your behalf.

It should take about two months from starting to look for a property until you are putting in an offer, and another two months from making an offer to exchange of contracts, and from then to completion – ie when you are free to move into the house – will be about another month. This time-guide depends very much on the state of the market when you are buying, and the whole thing could take much longer. It will also depend on whether or not you are taking out a mortgage. There is also the danger of being 'gazumped', which takes up time and often means that you have to start all over again.

In England and Wales the seller can choose to accept more than one offer. So even if your offer is accepted, it may not be the only one. If a higher offer comes along the agent's job is to pass it on to the seller, and it is up to the seller to decide whether or not to accept. Gazumping is when the seller gets an offer higher than the one he has accepted from you, and says that if you don't match it, he will sell to the higher bidder.

If the whole process of buying and selling were quicker, gazumping would be less likely to happen. This is not such a problem in Scotland because there the time between an offer being accepted and exchange of contracts is much less than in England and Wales.

If you are a 'cash buyer', ie not looking for a mortgage, you are obviously in a strong position to move ahead quickly with the purchase of the property. If you are gazumped, or find that you are involved in a race to exchange contracts, there is nothing you can do as you have no legal rights against the seller until you have exchanged contracts.

Buying a House in Scotland
In Scotland sales are often handled by solicitor's agents rather than estate agents. Basically they do the same job as estate agents but they will, on behalf of the buyer, contact local authorities as early as possible to get the equivalent of English local authority searches and enquiries carried out. When properties are advertised in Scotland it is usually stated that an offer over a certain figure will be considered up to a given date. If a buyer wants to get a structural survey done he should do so before making his offer because, if the offer is accepted, he will have to proceed immediately to a binding contract. The buyer's solicitor submits your offer in writing, stating the price being offered for the property, what is covered by the price, and the date the buyer wants to pay and move in. The offer may be accepted but with some proposed changes to some of the terms. Letters will go to and fro until a final agreement is reached. Once the buyer and seller formally agree a price and the other terms, they are legally bound to stick to the agreement. The buyer does not pay a deposit when the contract is made, but the full purchase price is payable when he moves in.

Getting a Mortgage
An Executive Mortgage
If you are a high earner you may be able to borrow a higher than normal multiple of salary. Some lenders allow you to put off paying part of the interest due, in a type of low-start scheme. It is advisable to check the income multiples available elsewhere. The cost is usually, but not invariably, the lender's normal rate.

A LIBOR-linked Mortgage
LIBOR is the London Inter-Bank Offered Rate. This type of mortgage has the interest rate fixed at a set percentage, usually 1 per cent above three-month LIBOR, the rate at which banks lend money to each other. There are financial risks involved in

a LIBOR mortgage; you can't forecast how it will compare with other mortgage rates.

An Interest-Only Mortgage
This is a mortgage where you pay interest to the lender but don't repay capital until the end of the loan. It is sometimes possible to borrow money on this basis without a set term for repaying the loan (or with only a nominal term), and without you being asked to pay premiums for a pension or endowment policy to pay off the loan.

The Fixed Interest Mortgage
These have the interest rate fixed for a certain period, at the rate obtaining when you take out the loan. There is a risk involved here in that, if interest rates go down, you will be left paying interest at above the going rate. On the other hand you could be lucky because if interest rates go up, you pay less than many other people. You may be penalised if you want to swap to a new lender, or to a variable rate before the end of the fixed period.

7
Education

The Education System in the UK
It is obviously important for the businessman bringing his family to stay in the UK to be aware of the various kinds of education which are on offer.

Education is compulsory in the UK for children between the ages of five and sixteen. There are also many opportunities for children to go to school before the age of five and, later, to enter institutions for higher education including universities and polytechnics. State schools are free.

Primary Schools
These usually provide education from five to the age of eleven, at which time children in England, Northern Ireland and Wales usually transfer to secondary schools. Some local authorities in England have established 'first' schools for children aged from five to eight or more, and 'middle' schools for those aged from eight to fourteen. In Scotland, primary school provides education from five to twelve years.

Secondary Schools
By far the greatest percentage of secondary education in England and Wales takes place at comprehensive schools. These can be organised in several ways. Some district schools take the pupil from eleven right through to eighteen years of age; others have middle schools whose pupils transfer at the age of twelve, thirteen or fourteen to a senior comprehensive, leaving at sixteen or eighteen.

Another alternative is a school with an age range of eleven to sixteen, combined with a sixth-form or tertiary college for pupils aged over sixteen. The latter provides a full range of vocational as well as academic courses, which prepare the student for further higher education.

Besides comprehensive schools there are 'grammar' and

'secondary modern' schools. Pupils are allotted to these schools after selection procedures at the age of eleven, when they have completed their primary schooling. These schools are not under the auspices of local education authorities but are managed by governing bodies funded from central government. Scottish state schools are mainly comprehensive, providing six-year courses, though there are some that only provide courses of four years' duration or less. In the latter case pupils may transfer to a six-year comprehensive school at the end of their second or fourth year.

Special Schools
Children with physical or mental handicaps, and emotionally disturbed children, can receive an education in some 1900 special schools, which include many run by voluntary organisations. Every effort is made in England, Scotland, Wales and Northern Ireland to see that many children with special needs are educated in ordinary schools, so that they do not feel they are different from other children. Special consideration is given to the parents' wishes and the needs of the pupil, as well as to the need for an efficient education for the other pupils in the school and for the efficient use of the school's resources.

Private Education
The cost of private education in the UK is high and rising, but the number of children attending fee-paying schools is on the increase. Fees range from in excess of £1,500 per annum for the cheapest preparatory school to nearly £10,000 for the more expensive senior boarding school. School fees have to be paid out of your after-tax income. The fees do not include the cost of the uniform and sports equipment, or school meals (except at boarding schools) and transport and other extras.

As more people are sending their children to fee-paying schools, so more insurance companies and brokers have seen that their products can be used to provide future school fees and now offer a 'school fees plan package'. This is basically a way of investing your money in order to be able to meet fees at a future date. In fact the majority of parents meet fees out of their earnings.

If you decide on a fee-paying school for your child, find out what the yearly fees are going to be. Then work out the monthly cost, to see what effect this will have on your monthly income, taking into account your other out-goings. It is possible that you will have to pay a term in advance, and so you will need to budget for this. If you decide you can afford a fee-paying school, it is wise to save as much as you can before the child starts attending the school and to set aside at least one term's fees in a deposit account or building society.

In your own country you may find that your employer, or professional association or trade union can offer help with school fees for the children of employees or members posted to work in the UK. However, it is possible that this help may be regarded as a fringe benefit for tax purposes. People in their country's diplomatic service may find that they are eligible for help with fees from their own government.

Boarding Schools
Sometimes parents who have to move around in their work find it best to stabilise their children's education by sending them to boarding school, and only having them back during the holidays. This is possible with private education but not necessarily advisable, as boarding school does not suit all children.

Getting More Information
Parents who are interested in sending their children to an independent private school would be well advised to purchase the publication *Which School?* It is a directory of independent schools of all types, listing over 2,300 schools throughout the UK, including independent day and boarding schools, public schools, Roman Catholic schools and special schools, as well as institutes of further and higher education, tutorial colleges, schools of English as a foreign language, secretarial colleges, nursery training colleges, and commercial/professional training establishments. It provides a geographical classification, with maps, which gives the location of the listed schools. There is a standard entry for each establishment giving information on, for example, the age range of pupils and the fees.

The book is published by Gabbitas, Truman and Thring Educational Trust, Broughton House, 6-8 Sackville Street,

77

Piccadilly, London W1X 2BR (Tel 071-734 0160 or 071-439 2071). It is now enjoying its sixty-fifth edition and is the only educational reference work of its kind published in a single volume. There is also information available on scholarships, the Assisted Places Scheme (see below), and the existing examination system. The trust has developed a range of more specialised guides giving information on specific types of education. So far three have been published: *Boarding Schools and Colleges; A Guide to Independent Further Education* and a *Guide to English Language Schools and Courses.*

The trust also runs an advisory service which offers guidance on a full range of educational opportunities from pre-school to university and beyond. It maintains a database which provides information not only on a wide range of British schools, but also on European schools. The advisory service not only obtains information regularly from schools and colleges but its staff also make regular visits, which enables them to assess the character of a particular establishment.

Scholarships and Financial Support
Many schools offer scholarships to academically gifted children, as well as to those with musical or artistic ability, and these can help substantially with fees. It is worth getting as much information as you possibly can. To find out more about scholarships, contact the Independent Schools Information Service (ISIS), 56 Buckingham Gate, London SW1E 6AG (Tel: 071-630 8795). If you and your partner have a joint gross income which is below a certain limit, it is worth finding out about the Assisted Places Scheme. This can help with fees at selected senior schools for entry at eleven, thirteen or sixteen years of age. Full information on the Assisted Places Scheme can be got from the Department of Education and Science, Room 3/65, Elizabeth House, York Road, London SE1 7PH (Tel: 071-934 9211); from the Welsh Office, Education Department, Cathays Park, Cardiff CF1 3NQ (Tel: 0222 823347); or from The Secretary, The Scottish Department, New St Andrew's House, Edinburgh EH1 3SY (Tel: 031-556 8400). You can get more information on school fees plans from banks, insurance companies and insurance brokers, and from certain building societies and unit trust managers.

The British Insurance Brokers Association, BIBA House, 14 Bevis Marks, London EC3A 7NT can give you a list of brokers in your area.

English Language Colleges

If your English needs improving, it is obviously better to take a language course before you leave home. However, if it is not possible to arrange this you will find that there are language schools throughout the UK offering a wide variety of courses to suit all needs and levels of ability, from the complete beginner to the technician needing specialist vocabulary. The long-term courses offer students the opportunity to study for a wide variety of internationally recognised examinations, and there are also a number of organisations offering short vacation courses which combine study with a holiday atmosphere.

Finding the Right Course for You

Language schools in Britain have a programme of social and leisure activities, excursions to places of interest, sports and outdoor activities. Modern teaching methods and audio-visual equipment are in use in most of the schools, and classes tend to have between ten and fifteen students so everyone gets some individual attention. Some schools offer one-to-one tuition with courses which will be organised to suit your particular requirements.

A list of schools recognised by the British Council is available from The British Council, 10 Spring Gardens, London SW1A 2BN. Schools on this list will have had their teaching services, premises, and student care and welfare service inspected. The British Council also publishes a series of information sheets under the general title 'English Studies Information Service'. You can get this series from your local British Council office. A number of British universities and colleges of further, higher and extended education also offer English language courses for overseas students, ranging from part-time courses for au pair students and visitors from overseas working in Britain, to summer vacation courses and full-time examination courses. These institutions are open to government inspection.

The British Association of State Colleges in English Language Teaching is a group of state-sector colleges, which is within the control of the Department of Education and Science. Its aim is to promote high standards of teaching, teacher training and student welfare. A list of its members can be obtained from the secretary of the association at Central Square, Hampstead Garden Suburb, London NW11 7BN.

The British Tourist Authority publishes a guide to English language schools and courses, *Learning English*. You can get a copy of this free from your local BTA office (see list of names and addresses, Appendix 3). When you find the school or organisation which will suit you, write to ask for a copy of the prospectus. Some of these schools have representatives overseas and you can book your course before you leave home. The BTA office will have details of tour operators in your country who specialise in booking English courses in Britain.

Obviously the fees of private schools are higher than those for state-run courses.

Making the Necessary Arrangements
If you are going to be following a course of study while you are in Britain, you will need confirmation that you have a place on the course. The Immigration Department will want to see this confirmation when you arrive. It is therefore important to arrange the course first, before you fix anything else to do with your stay in Britain. There are usually fewer places on courses than there are people applying for them, so to give yourself the best chance allow plenty of time and apply early. It is best to begin your enquiries *at least eighteen months* before the course you want starts. Most courses begin in September or October.

Polytechnics, Colleges of Higher Education and Further Education
Polytechnics
There are thirty polytechnics in **England and Wales**. These offer higher education in the form of basic introductory courses, advanced short courses, and degree, diploma, professional and postgraduate courses. The polytechnics have close links with commerce and industry and the courses they offer reflect this, in that they cover a range of administration, business and social studies. Science, mathematics, engineering and technology account for a third of the courses. The arts also play an important

role, with the emphasis on languages, literature, music, drama and the visual arts. Courses at every level can be studied full-time or part-time, during the day or evening. The polytechnics welcome enquiries from mature students who may need a pattern of study which takes account of childcare and other domestic commitments. A free leaflet listing the courses in all thirty polytechnics is available from CDP, Kirkman House, 12/14 Whitfield Street, London W1P 6AX (Tel: 071-637 9939).

In **Scotland** similar provision is made in the fifteen central institutions and in a number of further education colleges. In **Northern Ireland** courses are offered by the University of Ulster.

Colleges of Higher Education
A large number of students come to these institutions as a result of the integration of teacher-training colleges with the rest of higher education.

Further Education Colleges
These cater for students aged sixteen and over. They offer non-advanced courses as well as some specialised courses.

Universities
There are forty-seven universities in Britain, including the Open University. They have complete academic freedom. They appoint their own staff, decide which students to admit, what and how to teach, and which degrees to award. The two most famous universities in the UK are Oxford and Cambridge, which date from the twelfth and thirteenth centuries. The Scottish universities of St Andrews, Glasgow, Aberdeen and Edinburgh date mainly from the fifteenth and sixteenth centuries. All other universities in the UK were founded in the nineteenth and twentieth centuries. Admission is by examination or selection. At the present time there are approximately thirty thousand full-time university teachers paid wholly from university funds, and the ratio of full-time staff to full-time students is about 1 to 11, one of the most favourable in the world.

The Open University
This non-residential university provides degree and other courses for adult students of all ages throughout Britain. Students must normally be resident in the UK, but undergraduate courses are also available to English-speakers in Belgium, Luxembourg and the Netherlands. The Open University has advised many countries on setting up similar institutions.

University Study Holidays
A stay at a famous university, combining a holiday with study, is a very good way of acquiring new knowledge and skills and of getting to know people. The price of university study holidays usually includes full-board accommodation for seven days, all tuition, excursions to places of interest, and evening activities. You can usually arrange to bring a friend or partner and enjoy the experience together. If your partner does not wish to participate in the actual course, there is a reduction in the overall cost.

These week-long courses run from July to September and a very wide range of subjects is covered, including arts and literature; human interest, which explores such areas as alternative medicine; countryside courses, which examine English gardens, geology, and ornithology; and heritage courses. The visitor will surely find courses to suit his or her particular interests. The courses change slightly and are added to from year to year, so it is worth getting information direct from the university of your choice or alternatively from your local travel agent.

8

Insurance and Health

Insurance

You can find out about insurance from insurance firms or brokers and from banks, or if you are a student, from the Students' Union office at your college. There are often special student schemes which are less expensive.

It is advisable to have personal accident insurance, as well as personal property insurance to cover your personal effects and any contents of your accommodation which belong to you. If you are going to be using a bicycle, make sure that it is insured, if it is not included in your main insurance policy.

If you are not entitled to medical treatment under the National Health Service, remember private medical treatment is expensive; the cost of operations and hospitalisation can run into thousands of pounds. So take out medical insurance as soon as possible or, better still, arrange a satisfactory travel and health insurance before leaving home.

If you intend to drive a car in Britain you will need a valid driving licence, and the car must be registered, insured and taxed. When you buy the vehicle you should complete the transfer of ownership section on the registration document and, if the car is not taxed, get an application form from the Post Office for a vehicle road tax disc. With the completed form you will need to provide the registration document, the current insurance certificate and, if the car is over three years old, a current Ministry of Transport (MOT) test certificate of roadworthiness (approximately £15 and obtained from a garage), plus payment of the duty, currently £100 for a private car. Cars are usually taxed for six months or twelve months at a time, so, if the car is taxed when you buy it, check the expiry date and keep a note of it. You should also keep a note of your insurance and MOT certificate expiry dates as driving a car without the correct documents can carry heavy penalties. The tax disc must be displayed in the car front window.

Health

Britain's National Health Service (NHS), although sometimes criticised by the British themselves, is still the best of its kind in the world. The NHS is financed and run by the government. Those who live and work permanently in the UK are eligible for the entire range of NHS treatment. It is free, although there are some charges for medicines, dental treatment and dentures, glasses and some other appliances. Most accident, emergency and community services (not including hospitalisation) are free to everyone.

Are you Eligible for Treatment?

If you are in Britain as a student and are taking a course which lasts longer than six months, or if you come from an EC country, you will be eligible for treatment under the NHS. If you are here on an award administered by the British Council, your programme officer will advise you on what facilities are available to you.

You will also be eligible for free treatment if you come from one of the countries listed below, as they have reciprocal health agreements with Britain: Anguilla, Australia, Austria, Belgium, British Virgin Islands, Bulgaria, Channel Islands, Czechoslovakia, Falkland Islands, Finland, German Democratic Republic, German Federal Republic, Gibraltar, Greece, Hong Kong, Hungary, Iceland, Irish Republic, Isle of Man, Israel, Italy, Malta, Montserrat, Netherlands, New Zealand, Norway, Poland, Portugal, Romania, Spain, St Helena, Sweden, Turks and Caicos Islands, Union of Soviet Socialist Republics, and Yugoslavia.

How to Register for NHS Treatment

Anyone eligible for free NHS treatment is also entitled to register with a doctor. You should always go to your doctor first for treatment, except in an emergency when you should go straight to the casualty department of a hospital or phone for an ambulance by dialling 999.

If you are entitled to register with an NHS doctor you should do so as soon as possible after you arrive in this country. Please do not wait until you are ill. You can get a list of NHS doctors – usually called GPs (General Practitioners) – from the local Family Practitioner Committee, the local Community Health Council (in Scotland this is the local Health Board or Health Council, and in Northern Ireland the Central Services Agency), the Citizen's Advice Bureau, main Post Offices and from public libraries (addresses in the telephone directory). The list will not tell you much about the doctor, so to find one you think will suit you ask local people or, if you are a student, ask at your college. Universities and colleges sometimes have their own Student Health Service. It is wise to choose a doctor who is easy to get to when you are not feeling well.

Once you have decided on a doctor, visit the surgery and ask to be put on the list of patients. If the doctor is able to accept you, you will be asked to complete an application form. In due course you will be sent your medical or NHS card, which will carry your NHS number. It is important to keep this safely as you will need to produce the card or quote the number when using other parts of the NHS.

If you have difficulty getting a doctor to accept you – and in certain parts of the country this can happen even to permanent residents – you must contact the Family Practitioner Committee, which is obliged to see that you are placed on a doctor's list. Once you have sorted this out you should let someone reliable at your place of work or your college have your doctor's name, address and telephone number, in case of an emergency.

Getting an Appointment
If you need to visit the surgery, check surgery hours first. These can vary but there is usually a morning and/or early evening surgery on weekdays. Often emergency cases are seen on a Saturday. Many doctors operate an appointment system so you should telephone in advance and make an appointment. There is an emergency telephone number to ring when the surgery is closed.

As most doctors are extremely busy you will find that, unless you are too ill to travel, you will have to attend the surgery in person to get treatment. If you have to have a home visit you should ring the surgery, or get someone else to do this for you, and describe your symptoms. It is useful to ring as early as

85

possible in the morning so that the doctor can plan to fit you in later in the day, when he goes out on his rounds.

The doctor will prescribe any medication you may need. Take the prescription to the nearest chemist or, if it is after normal opening hours, ask the doctor's receptionist for the name of a chemist open at that time. A list of chemists which are open late and at weekends is available from your local chemist's shop. There is a flat rate prescription charge at the moment of approximately £3 for each medicine. In Britain few drugs are available without a doctor's prescription.

If necessary, the doctor will refer you to a hospital for specialist treatment, blood tests, x-rays etc. The hospital will decide whether your treatment can be provided under the NHS.

Private Medicine
If you are not entitled to register with a doctor under the NHS, you will have to be a private patient and pay for each visit and the full cost of all medicines prescribed. Some NHS doctors take private patients, and most dentists will. Private doctors and dentists will also be listed in the *Yellow Pages* telephone directory for your area.

Even if you are in the country for less than six months you will not be charged for immediate treatment at hospital casualty departments, or for treatment of certain communicable diseases which confine you to hospital. However, if you have to be admitted to hospital after an accident or in an emergency, or if you need to return for further treatment, you will be charged.

If you are in Britain for a study course lasting more than six months your dependants will also be able to get treatment for illnesses which arise here. However, anyone who comes to the UK with the specific aim of having treatment whilst here may have to pay for private treatment. Relatives or friends who visit you for a short period of time during your studies will not be considered as dependants, and they will need to be covered by private medical insurance.

Private Medical Insurance
Many citizens within the UK take out private medical insurance because it enables a person to have an unessential operation, such as a replacement hip, without having to go on a

long waiting list. Unfortunately NHS patients now frequently have to go on such lists.

A word of warning – many of the private medical insurance companies, when asked to pay out, will scrupulously research your case in order to see if they consider themselves obliged to pay or whether your problem can be said to be the result of some former weakness.

Spas and Health Farms

Many people are interested in visiting spas for rehabilitation after an operation, accident or sports injury, or as a more natural method of treating rheumatology or arthritis, or simply to lose weight and get fit. Finding the right place for treatment of particular problems requires expert advice. Fortunately there is an organisation in the UK called Erna Low Consultants Limited which specialises in this service. The address is 9 Reece Mews, London SW7 3HE (Tel: 071-584 2841).

The company offers help in two ways. Firstly, it can arrange for you to talk to a specialist spa doctor to discuss your problem in confidence and decide on the best centre for the treatment you need. Secondly, wherever that centre is – whether in Britain or on the Continent – Erna Low Consultants makes the necessary travel and accommodation arrangements in accordance with your wishes, needs and budget.

For a long period British spas have been neglected, although they were very popular with the Romans and also in Georgian times. Nowadays British spas are in the process of redevelopment and arrangements are being made for guests and patients to stay in Bath, Royal Leamington Spa, Matlock Spa and Droitwich Spa.

Unlike spas, health farms have been increasing in popularity in the UK over the past few years because the British have become very health-conscious in recent times. And these places are excellent for preventive medicine, such as relieving stress symptoms and adjusting weight problems, which are frequently found to be the manifestation of some brewing emotional unrest.

Among these health centres and resorts is one of the world's best, Champneys in Tring, set high above the Vale of Aylesbury. Others in the south, south-west and Midlands of England

87

include Grayshott Hall in Surrey, Shrubland Hall in Suffolk, Cedar Falls in Somerset, Forest Mere in Hampshire, Henlow Grange in Bedfordshire, Tyringham in Buckinghamshire, and Springs Hydro in Leicestershire. In Scotland and the north of England are Roundel Wood at Crieff and Brooklands Country House in Lancashire. In Wales there is the Snowdonian National Park Health Lodge.

Again it should be stressed that specialist knowledge is essential to establish the best place for the individual's requirements. If this place cannot be found in the UK, Erna Low Consultants has contacts with leading spas and health resorts in Switzerland at Lenk, St Moritz, Leukerbad, Bad Ragaz, Baden bei Zurich, and Vevey; in France, with Thalassotherapy Centres in Brittany, – Roscoff, Pervos Guirec, St Malo, Quiberon, Carnac, Le Touquet, Deuville, as well as the Helianthal Spa and Leisure Hotel at St Jean de Luz, and in the spa town of Vichy; in Italy, with health resorts and thermal centres in Obano and Montegrotto, Sirmion, Montecatini and Ischia; in Germany, with such famous spas as Baden-Baden, Bad Ems and Bad Toetz; and in Austria, with Baden bei Wien and Badgastein. It also has contacts with spas in Yugoslavia, Czechoslovakia and Hungary, which have very favourable exchange rates for sterling.

Some medical health schemes in Europe include these forms of treatment as part of the country's national health scheme, and citizens receive a contribution towards treatment. In Britain, spa and health centre courses are not part of the NHS but many businesses send staff for treatment at the company's expense, particularly those members who are showing signs of stress. Also, many companies book conference facilities at hotels which offer health treatment, such as the Mirador in Vevey and the Royal Hotel in Scarborough.

Contraception and Getting Advice

Contraception and birth control advice are available free to those who are eligible for treatment under the NHS. You can either go to your own doctor, or to a local NHS Family Planning Clinic. Condoms are not available free under the NHS but may be bought at chemists' and often in other shops.

If you should become pregnant, go to your doctor, a Family

Planning Clinic or, if you are a student, your college for advice. There is plenty of help and support available while you decide what to do. An unmarried pregnant woman in Britain receives exactly the same sort of help and advice as a married woman. Do not delay in asking for advice.

You can also get advice on contraception, pregnancy and abortion from some private agencies which are registered with the Department of Health and Social Security (DHSS). These include the British Pregnancy Advisory Service, Austy Manor, Wootton Warren, Solihull, West Midlands B95 6BX (Tel: 05642 3225); and the Pregnancy Advisory Service, 11/13 Charlotte Street, London SW1 (Tel: 071 638 8962).

Well Woman Clinics
In some parts of the country Well Woman Clinics have been set up. These deal specifically with all aspects of women's health. Your local health clinic or your doctor will be able to tell you if there is one in the area where you live, and there will also be information at the public library. Well Woman Clinics are not usually listed in the telephone directory.

Sexually Transmitted Diseases
As their name implies, sexually transmitted diseases are avoidable. The only sure way of avoiding venereal disease (VD), which is the most widespread contagious disease in the world, is not to have sex, particularly casual sex with someone whom you don't know. A booklet, available from the Health Education Council, 78 New Oxford Street, London WC1, lists the symptoms and gives advice on what action to take if you think you have contracted such a disease. Advice will also be available from your nearest Family Planning Clinic. VD can be cured if it is treated early.

AIDS
Aids is now present worldwide and there is as yet no vaccine and no cure for it. It is fatal. It is caused by a virus called HIV. All those infected by the virus are at risk of developing AIDS, but even those who do not develop full-blown AIDS will remain infected and infectious all their lives. You cannot catch the virus from everyday contact with other people, for example from

swimming pools, food or crockery. You can catch it by having sex with an infected man or woman, or if blood contaminated by the virus gets into your body. The virus can be passed by an infected mother to her baby before, during or shortly after childbirth. People can be infectious to others even if they look and feel completely well themselves.

It therefore makes sense to protect yourself. Do not have casual sex. If you do, use a condom. Do not inject illegal drugs. The sharing of infected needles and equipment is a major cause of the spread of the virus. If you must inject, never share. If at any time during your stay you are worried about AIDS and would like to talk to someone in confidence, you can call the National AIDS Helpline any time, free of charge. The number is 0800 567 123.

Dentists

It is now necessary to register with a dentist. As you may need to see a dentist at some point during your stay, it is worth finding and registering with one who will treat you under the NHS – many dentists see both private and NHS patients.

Your main Post Office will have a list of local dentists. When making your appointment ask if treatment is possible under the NHS, and quote your NHS number. There is a flat charge for dental treatment under the NHS (less than £20), but this is a lot less than private treatment will cost. You will need to make an appointment well in advance as most NHS dentists are very busy, but if you are in pain the dentist will try to see you that day.

Opticians

If you think you should have your eyes tested, or if your doctor suggests it, you may go to any optician for an eye test. Your local main Post Office or library will have a list of registered opticians in your area, or look in the *Yellow Pages* phone book under 'Opticians'.

Eye tests are not free under the NHS except to certain categories of people (for instance, diabetics), and the costs vary from one optician to another, so it may pay you to shop around. The test will cost in the region of £10 and it you need spectacles you will be charged separately for lenses and frames. The price of frames also varies widely so do enquire about the full price range. You are not under any obligation to buy your lenses and frames from, ie have the prescription made up by, the optician who tests your sight – again, you can shop around. The prescription is your property.

Healthcall Directory
If you have any worries about your health, it is worth bearing in mind the *Healthcall Directory*. You can get a free copy by phoning 0898 600 600. This gives access to a totally confidential library of medical information which operates 24 hours a day. You look up the subject in which you are interested in the directory, dial the telephone number beside it, and wait for the tape to start playing. It takes about 20sec to be connected.

9

Transport

The Railway System

The first railway passenger line was built in England from Stockton to Darlington in 1825. The Darlington Railway Centre and Museum attracts visitors from all over the world who come to see George Stephenson's No 1 *Locomotion* which pulled the original train at the speed of 21kmph (13mph). Things developed apace from then on, and in 1833 Isambard Kingdom Brunel was asked to construct a railway line from London to Bristol. Over the following decades Britain established an enormous transport network, which took most of the nation's traffic off the canals and onto the railways and seduced passengers away from the stagecoach onto passenger trains. Meanwhile railway engineers from Britain went all over the world to help build trains and railways on other continents.

Up until 1947 four large railway companies ran the railway network in Great Britain, and then the Transport Act brought them under public ownership. It is now expected that they will soon be privatised again. In 1962 the British Railways Board was set up to manage railway affairs and subsidiary activities. The board manages most of the railway network in Great Britain, except for the Underground systems in London and Glasgow, the Tyne and Wear Metro and a few stretches of private line. On the passenger side, the company's main businesses are InterCity, Network SouthEast and Provincial Services. Two other business sectors look after Railfreight and Parcels.

In Britain there are 17,500km (approximately 11,000 miles) of rail network and 2,500 stations, enabling the passenger to visit historic cities like Edinburgh, York, Canterbury and Stratford-upon-Avon, and to pass through scenic countryside ranging from the vales and dales of England and Wales to the Scottish Highlands. In Northern Ireland the Northern Ireland Railways Company operates a railway service on some 300km (184 miles) of track. In Britain today, some 165 years after the construction of the first line, the train still remains one of the main ways of getting to and from business, visiting friends and relatives, and seeing the country.

When you buy your ticket, you buy a ride on the train but not necessarily a seat. Throughout the day there are usually so many trains running between different destinations that seats are almost always available to passengers, but this is not the case in rush hours and peak periods. Therefore, if you are travelling a long distance at a peak period – a Friday evening or Sunday evening all year round, or on a public holiday or during summer vacations – it is advisable for the sake of comfort to reserve a seat in advance, for which there is a small payment of £1 standard class and £2 first class.

Having purchased a ticket it is necessary to retain it, as it will probably be examined again on the train and then have to be handed in at the barrier after the journey. It costs considerably more to purchase a ticket on the train than at the ticket office in the station at the start of your journey. However, stations on some rural lines do not have ticket offices. In this case it is usual to buy a ticket on the train and the normal price will be charged.

Good Deals
One of the best deals for the incoming visitor is to purchase a BritRail pass, which allows unlimited travel for four, eight, fifteen or twenty-two days in a month at a very competitive price. You can also buy a pass for every day of the month, but all BritRail passes must be purchased prior to departure for the UK.

The BritRail Gold Pass covers first-class travel and the Silver Pass covers standard-class travel. Further deductions are available for people over sixty or under twenty-six years of age. Visitors should not confuse Eurail passes (which are not valid in Britain) with BritRail passes. Details and prices of these offers are available from BR's international offices or the offices of general sales agents abroad, listed in Appendix 2. Most of these outlets are close to existing overseas British Tourist Authority offices.

There are many money-saving offers from British Rail. Most of them involve travelling at less busy periods. If you wish to make use of these Savers, you usually have to be prepared to travel outside the rush hour and not on Fridays. Full information on Savers can be obtained from any station ticket office, provided you ask for it. Never buy a ticket without first making sure you are getting the best deal for your pocket and your purposes.

Other savings are available for students who purchase a Young Person's Railcard, which provides discounts on a whole range of fare structures. The same sort of offer applies to people over sixty years of age, who purchase a Senior Citizen's Railcard. Likewise, there is a Family Railcard which allows great savings when children and adults are travelling together.

At weekends it is possible to upgrade from standard accommodation to first class for only £3 extra, and by booking ahead you can also get a free seat reservation.

The purchase of a Rail Rover ticket enables people on holiday to see the country at a reduced cost. The tickets are available either for the whole network or specific regions.

Getting Information
On arriving in Britain, visitors will find British Rail Travel Centres in most terminals at the major international airports. Here you can obtain assistance and information regarding onward journeys.

Besides the international airports, all major mainline stations throughout Britain have a travel centre or an information kiosk, and local stations will nearly all have a ticket sales counter. Here you can also obtain a rail map. Easy-to-understand route schedules display times of arrival and departure of local trains. If you are travelling a long distance, you will probably have to travel through one of the nine mainline London stations and the railmap will show which station to travel through to reach your selected destination.

InterCity, or Letting the train take the strain
British Rail's Intercity operation is the flagship of its business. InterCity trains carry 200,000 passengers every day, with a fast and frequent service between cities from Aberdeen and Inverness in the north to Poole and Penzance in

the south. There are direct links to most of the international UK airports, such as Gatwick, Birmingham and Manchester, and it is expected that these services will continue to increase and improve. The InterCity service clocks up some 13.6 billion passenger kilometres (8½ billion passenger miles) annually.

Frequent high speed services run at regular intervals over all the principal routes in InterCity's 6,035km (3,750 mile) national network. On many shorter-distance routes, for example London to Birmingham and London to Leicester, you will find there is a half-hourly service for much of the day. Hourly services operate on most other main routes. These include routes from London (Paddington) to Swindon, Bristol and South Wales, as well as to Exeter, Plymouth and Cornwall; from London (Euston) to Crewe, Preston, Carlisle and Glasgow, as well as to Birmingham and Wolverhampton, and to Manchester and to Liverpool; from London (St Pancras) to Leicester, Nottingham, Derby and Sheffield; from London (King's Cross) to York, Newcastle, Edinburgh and Aberdeen as well as to Doncaster and Leeds; and from London (Liverpool Street) to Ipswich and Norwich.

Most InterCity trains have buffet cars where the passenger can purchase a snack and alcoholic and non-alcoholic beverages, and many of the long-distance trains have restaurant cars. British Rail is famous for its hearty English breakfasts, and there is a good selection of wines with lunch and dinner. First and standard-class sleepers can be reserved at extra cost on many overnight trains. Cars can be taken on some long-haul trains and enquiries regarding this should be made to Motorail.

Recently British Rail has developed a new network of modern Super Sprinter trains, which have the word Sprinter printed on them. These services have cut travelling time for many cross-country routes because they link directly major towns and cities in different regions, and the traveller does not have to make his way to London to begin his or her journey.

At present Sprinters link north-west England to East Anglia. Services start from Liverpool and Blackpool, and then carry on to a range of East Anglian destinations. On the Birmingham to East Anglia run an hourly service links the West Midlands with Leicester, Peterborough and Ely, and then radiates out to East Anglia. There is a Sprinter every two hours from Cardiff in Wales to Manchester and one to Liverpool, giving an hourly service between Cardiff and Crewe – a major interchange station for London and Scotland. Two Sprinters per day link Cardiff with North Wales. An hourly service operates between Cardiff, Bristol, Bath, Salisbury, Southampton and Portsmouth, with two trains a day running through to Brighton. A two-hourly service operates between Cardiff and Birmingham and calls at Worcester and Cheltenham.

Other important links are from Scarborough and Hull to Liverpool and Manchester, which combined with another service from Newcastle to Liverpool provides a half-hourly service between Leeds and Manchester. Being aware of these particular regional services, which are increasing all the time, can save the traveller much time and money.

Land Cruises
InterCity offers fabulous Land Cruises whereby special trains, fitted out like luxury liners on wheels, take the visitor around different parts of Britain and provide sleeping accommodation and a high-quality restaurant on board.

The Land Cruises have three itineraries at the time of going to press. The West Highlander tour leaves from St Pancras station and goes up to Oban, visits the Isle of Mull and Iona and goes on to Fort William for an overnight hotel stop before continuing to Mallaig and Glenfinnan and enjoying a short cruise on Loch Nevis. The tours leave on a Friday evening and return Monday evening.

The Orcadian also leaves from St Pancras, goes to the most northerly railway junction, Georgemas, and then guests go on by road to John O'Groats and by ferry to the Orkneys, a domain inhabited first by the Celts and then by the Norsemen. On the return journey a visit is made to Skye, an island made famous by the exploits of Bonnie Prince Charlie. The tours leave on Friday afternoon and return on Monday morning.

The Scillonian leaves St Pancras and goes down into the Westcountry. The visitor has a choice of three tours, which include two to the nearly sub-tropical Isles of Scilly and a

(Above) *The traditional thatched-roof Olde English country pub at Drusillas in Sussex not only serves beer but is a recognised English wine centre, selling popular English vintages*
(Below) *British Rail Intercity 'Land Cruises' offer scenic tours of Britain. Here on the West Highland Line in Scotland, the train travels between Fort William and Mallaig*

(Above) *The parish church in Alderney, one of the Channel Islands, was designed by Sir Gilbert Scott in the transitional style from Norman to early English Cruciform*

(Right) *Cleeve Abbey, founded for Cistercian monks in 1188, is now an English Heritage monument. Seen here is the attractive gatehouse, built in 1530*

(Above) *Middlethorpe Hall in Yorkshire, a stately home restored to its former glory by Historic House Hotels, now offers luxury accommodation*

(Below) *Hartwell House in Buckinghamshire was leased to the French king Louis XVIII in the nineteenth century. It has recently been restored and is now a luxury hotel with conference facilities*

(Above) *This simple cottage in Alloway is where Robert Burns, Scotland's greatest bard, was born in 1759. It marks the start of the 'Burns Heritage Trail' originally conceived by the Scottish Tourist Board*
(Below) *The coastal town of Anstruther was once the main centre of the Scottish herring industry, and today is the home of the Scottish Fisheries Museum*

(Above) *Edinburgh, the capital of Scotland, with its famous castle*
(left) *where the Edinburgh Tattoo is held. The monument to Sir Walter
Scott* (right) *overlooks Princes Street*
(Below) *Wild and lonely, the Isle of Skye, with its awesome Cuillin
Mountains, is immortalised in the Scottish ballad to Bonnie Prince
Charlie,* Over the Sea to Skye

(Above) *Conwy, with its ancient castle and contoured enceinte of high town walls, is a major holiday attraction on the coast of north-west Wales*
(Below) *One of several narrow guage railways in Wales restored by enthusiast, the Brecon Mountain Railway steam train takes visitors through Brecon Beacon's National Park*

A coracle on the River Teifi in Wales. It is constructed of intertwined laths of willow and hazel to a design that has changed little since ancient times

third to Land's End peninsula. The train leaves on a Tuesday evening and returns Thursday night. For further information on costs and times of travel, contact either InterCity Land Cruise Booking Office, 104 Buckingham Road, Lichfield, Staffs WS14 9BW, or the British Rail Travel Centre, Euston Station, London.

One-Day Excursions
In addition to Land Cruises, InterCity has a summer programme of a dozen luxury days out – trips to beauty spots or places of historic interest throughout Britain, with meals on board. In comparison with the standard rail fare, the prices for these are very competitive. Bookings can be made at the British Rail Travel Centre, Euston. Visitors to Britain wishing to take a holiday by rail would be interested in the InterCity brochure *A Guide to Holidaymaker Services*, and students who might like a holiday with bicycles should obtain the British Rail brochure, *The Rail Traveller's Guide to BIKING by Train*. It specifies many routes where you take your bike free.

A Trip to the Continent
British Rail International Services, which will no doubt grow in importance when the Channel Tunnel is completed and links Britain with the Continent, offers many interesting tours to other European countries.

For example, from London to Brussels – headquarters of the European Common Market as well as the home of NATO (North Atlantic Treaty Organisation) – there are four daily train/jetfoil services which average 5hr 15min from city centre to city centre. By the three daily train/ferry services the journey takes 7hr 45min. Costs by European Saver (five-day return fares) start from around £43 by ship and £56 by jetfoil, with substantial reductions in November. Even less expensive are journeys to the beautiful medieval canal cities of Bruges and Ghent, which are so popular with those fascinated by history, sightseeing and gourmet food.

Similar journeys also take travellers to Germany and the Netherlands. Bookings for these trips, depending on the final destination, can be made through the International Rail Centre at Victoria or the Travel Centre at Liverpool Street Station. Telephone 071-834 2345 for enquiries or 071-828 0892 for credit card bookings.

Inter-Rail Card

Students who wish to travel on the Continent of Europe during their holidays should be aware of the Inter-Rail card for those aged under twenty-six, which gives unlimited rail travel for one month through twenty-one countries for around £150. This ticket can be bought in Great Britain or Northern Ireland provided that you can prove that you have been resident in the UK for at least six months prior to purchase.

The Inter-Rail and Boat card costs £175 and offers all the facilities of the basic Inter-Rail card, plus free travel on some Mediterranean, Scandinavian and Irish shipping routes.

A Trip to Ireland

European InterCity offers an economical way of travelling to Ireland by rail and ferry. The ferry routes across include Stranraer to Belfast, Liverpool to Belfast, Holyhead to Dun Laoghaire, and Fishguard to Rosslare.

Travel by Road

There are four types of road in the United Kingdom, motorways, 'A' roads, 'B' roads, and 'unclassified' roads. All of them except unclassified roads are marked on most road maps. Motorways are usually marked in blue, 'A' roads usually in red and 'B' roads usually in green.

There are approximately 378,150km (234,970 miles) of public road, of which 3,000km (1,860 miles) are trunk motorways, which usually have three lanes running in either direction. Public roads in England cover 270,265km (168,916 miles), in Scotland 51,206km (32,004 miles), in Wales 32,842km (20,526 miles), and in Northern Ireland 23,838km (14,899 miles). Among these, England has 2,537km (1,586 miles) of motorway, Scotland has 233km (146 miles), Wales has 119km (74 miles), and Northern Ireland 111km (70 miles).

Nearly 24 million vehicles are licensed for use on British roads and the number is still growing year by year. Hence, there are schemes afoot worth several million pounds to extend and increase the number of motorways.

Private Motoring

In the UK the easiest way to get around is often to get into one's car and drive from door to door. If you decide to buy and use a car for this purpose, there are certain important items and useful tips to bear in mind. Firstly, acquire an International Driving Permit before leaving home. It is not always essential to have one, as current driving licences issued by foreign countries are valid up to twelve months in this country, but the international permit is a wise investment. Purchase from Her Majesty's Stationery Office (HMSO), or a stationery shop such as W.H. Smith's, a copy of *The Highway Code*, which will provide you with all the regulations you need to know regarding driving in the UK.

One of the most important things to remember is that we drive on the left. Most car steering wheels are on the right and this will help you to remember, but of course you won't have the reminder if you bring your own car and have steering on the left. The greatest danger for a person who is used to driving on the right-hand side is to go into a roundabout the wrong way. Remember to go round in a clockwise direction. Also, when approaching, give way to traffic actually on the roundabout. It is law that front seat passengers wear a seat belt. If you don't, you risk being fined.

Unless otherwise indicated, the speed limit in built-up areas is 48kmph (30mph) and this is usually signposted. 96kmph (60mph) is allowed on single carriageways and 112kmph (70mph) on motorways and dual carriageways. Although the UK has one of the highest densities of road traffic in the world, it also has one of the lowest road-accident death rates within the EC. This is due to a number of strict regulations and heavy penalties against drinking and driving, dangerous driving, and regarding vehicle maintenance. All visitors should acquaint themselves with these regulations.

Two motoring organisations in the UK offer a wide range of valuable services, and the motorist is advised to join one of them. They are the Automobile Association (AA), which has its headquarters at Fanum House, Basingstoke, Hampshire RG21

2EA (Tel: 0256 201123), and the Royal Automobile Club (RAC) with headquarters at 49 Pall Mall, London SW1Y 5JG (Tel: 071 839 7050).

Travel by Coach

There is a wide range of regional and local coach and bus services throughout Britain. These provide the cheapest category of transport. The main national coachline is National Express and it produces an encyclopaedic publication on routes, timetables and special offers.

National Express services criss-cross the UK and link 1,500 destinations nationwide. The services operate every day of the year except Christmas Day, throughout England, Wales and Scotland. They carry 14 million passengers every year and the longest route is 1,075km (668 miles) from Plymouth to Aberdeen.

Apart from featuring big at Victoria Coach Station at Buckingham Palace Road in London, National Express operates coach stations in Birmingham, Bournemouth, Manchester and Leeds. There are major interchange points at Birmingham, Bristol, Cambridge, Edinburgh, Glasgow, Leicester, Manchester, Nottingham, Preston and Sheffield. There are two key points where you can obtain information on coach services: contact The Coach Travel Centre, 13 Regent Street, London; or, in Scotland, Scottish Citylink at St Andrew Square Bus Station, Edinburgh.

Altogether there are 2,500 National Express agents throughout Britain, including bus company travel offices, your local travel agent, and certain village stores. Tickets can be bought at any of these venues and by credit card from most of the telephone enquiry centres. You should allow five days for tickets to be processed and sent on to your address in the UK.

National Express has two categories of coach service. The Rapide network offers the very best in express coach travel. Each coach carries a stewardess who will serve you with a full range of light refreshments, brought to your seat as in an aircraft. Each coach has reclining seats, individual ventilation, and a washroom with toilet. These services operate between most major cities, whereas normal services reach a much wider range of destinations. On the latter, refreshment and toilet stops are made every few hours, although many of the coaches are also fitted with their own washroom and toilet. You may buy your ticket from the driver.

Most National Express services operate at hourly or two-hourly intervals. Customers using the busy route between Birmingham and London have a Rapide service which runs half-hourly, and there are Rapide departure lounges at either end – Birmingham, Pavilions and London, Victoria Coach Station. The Birmingham Rapide Shuttle lounge is also available for passengers for coaches serving Leicester, Nottingham, Manchester Airport and Manchester. Both lounges offer comfortable seating and refreshments.

In the London area and Home Counties, London Express has a network of routes. Its coaches connect at Victoria Coach Station, twice every day, with the nationwide National Express network. This network provides certain interesting days out with visits to places such as Windsor Safari Park, Chessington Zoo, Leeds Castle, Wisley Gardens and Southend.

The Caledonian Express/Stagecoach offers direct day and overnight services between Aberdeen, Dundee, Inverness, Perth, Glasgow, Edinburgh and London. One example is service 840, which goes to Gatwick Airport, Heathrow Airport, London, Milton Keynes, Carlisle, Glasgow, Perth, Dundee, Aberdeen and Inverness.

Good Deals

As mentioned earlier, journeying by coach is the least expensive mode of travel and there are also certain special deals of which the visitor should be aware. The Britexpress Card, which costs £9, is available to all overseas visitors and allows a one-third discount on every journey made in a specified period of thirty consecutive days. It can be bought in your country of origin or on arrival in the UK.

The Tourist Trail Pass provides unlimited travel on National Express and Scottish Citylink services for any five, eight, fifteen, twenty-two or thirty-day period. Adult prices range from £48 for five days to £135 for thirty days. It is only available to the overseas visitor.

For all students in full-time education, there is a Young Person's Coach Card priced at £5 (at the time of going to press), which entitles the holder to one third off standard fares for a twelve-month period. Another discount fare is the 'Standby', which costs about 20 per cent less than a normal or reserved-seat fare; it is available on both one-way and return journeys. Below is a sample of some different return fare structures at the time of going to press.

	Economy	*With discount card*
London–Leeds	£19.50	£13.00
London–Manchester	£15.00	£9.00
London–Bristol	£12.00	£8.00

Coach Travel Vouchers which can be given as gifts can be obtained from National Express Headquarters at 4 Vicarage Road, Edgbaston, Birmingham B15 3ES in £1, £5 and £10 denominations.

Holidays by Coach
Holiday destinations reached by various coach services range from Falmouth in Cornwall to Inverness in the Scottish Highlands, with a choice of sixty-five other destinations in between.

To give some idea of cost, Frames offers an inclusive three-day tour of the English Lakes for £120 per person, Excelsior offers a four-day tour of North Wales and Snowdonia and the Wye Valley for £95, and Evans offers a four-day tour of Scotland for £215. These prices were correct at the time of going to press and, of course, costs vary according to distances and standard of accommodation.

National Express offers a wide range of bargain breaks, ranging from one-night stays in London to fifteen days at scenic resorts. Your local travel agent will be happy to supply you with ideas to choose from. Accommodation on these holiday breaks is aimed to suit all pockets and can vary from hotels and university halls of residence to self-catering in fully equipped caravans.

Northern Ireland
In Northern Ireland nearly all the road passenger services come under the auspices of the publicly owned Northern Ireland

Transport Holding Company. Citybus Limited operates services in the capital of Belfast, and Ulster-bus Limited provides services for the rest of Northern Ireland. Together they own and run some 1,350 vehicles.

The Continent
For travel in Europe, there is the Eurolines network of express coach services. This comprehensive network links the main towns and cities in France, Spain, Portugal, Germany, Italy, Belgium, the Netherlands, Turkey, Bulgaria, Morocco, Yugoslavia, Switzerland, Denmark, Sweden, Norway, Finland, Greece, Poland and Ireland. Most Eurolines coaches leave from Victoria Coach Station and therefore offer easy connections with National Express services throughout the UK.

Tickets for and information about Eurolines coach services can be obtained from National Express outlets. For telephone enquiries about Eurolines, phone 071 730 0202 or 0582 404511.

Travel by Air
There are around one hundred and forty licensed civil aerodromes in the UK, and altogether the civil airports deal with nearly one hundred million passengers a year. Eleven of the airports handle over a million passengers a year each.

Heathrow Airport
Heathrow, which lies 26km (16 miles) west of London close to the M4 and M25, is the largest international passenger airport in the world. It caters for aircraft belonging to seventy different airlines from all over the world and serving innumerable destinations. As a rule of thumb, all domestic and Irish flights come into Terminal 1, all European flights come into Terminal 2, and all intercontinental flights come into Terminal 3. Terminal 4 handles nearly all British Airways (BA) intercontinental flights into and out of Heathrow, including Concorde. This national airline travels to more foreign destinations than any other existing airline, serving as it does over one hundred and sixty destinations in some seventy-five countries.

There are exceptions to the rule of thumb just given. Terminal 1, as well as handling domestic and Irish flights (which include for instance Air UK, BA-UK Shuttle and Europe (not Paris and Amsterdam), British Midland, Brymon Airways, Dan-Air, Manx Airlines and Aer Lingus), also handles flights of certain other airlines, such as Cyprus Airways, El Al, Icelandair, Sabena Belgian Airlines, and South African Airways to and from overseas destinations.

Terminal 4, besides handling BA intercontinental flights and her flights to Paris, Amsterdam and Athens, also services Air Malta, KLM and NLM City Hopper.

Travel from Heathrow. Rail/Air coaches run regularly from Heathrow's four terminals to Reading station for trains to the west of England, South Wales and the Midlands. Outside the rush hour, the coach journey takes an hour along the M4 motorway.

The Rail/Air coach link runs half-hourly during the day and begins from Terminal 3, the Heathrow intercontinental terminal. Here the coach is parked before stopping outside each of the other termini. You will usually have to stand and wait at Terminal 3 until five minutes before coach departure for the driver to unlock and let you on, but don't worry, he will turn up. The times of departure are written up close by, so that if you wish to keep warm in the winter you can wait inside the terminal and come back. All termini display coach schedules. The money for your ticket is collected by conductors at Terminal 4. The fare is £9 for a monthly return, but only £5.50 for a day return. Singles are £4.50.

From Heathrow you can travel into London by Underground trains, which run every few minutes from early morning until nearly midnight. The Underground network will take you to any of the main railway stations feeding the rest of Britain.

Plans are afoot to open a fast express train service by 1993 between Heathrow and Paddington, which will only take twenty minutes from the airport to the centre of London. Metered taxis, which are expensive, will also take passengers into London.

Two Airbuses run regularly to British Rail stations at Euston and Victoria. There are also a host of other buses at the airport, including the Rail-Link bus to Woking for trains to Hampshire and Dorset, which will help the incoming visitor to reach his destination.

Other important coaches include the Speedlink service, which runs non-stop between Heathrow and Gatwick (approximately

£10 single fare), and the Jetlink 747 which connects Heathrow and Gatwick with another London airport at Luton. Express services to central London are operated by several companies including Flightline 767, which goes direct to Victoria Coach Station, which is the main coach station in London with services to destinations throughout Britain (approximately £7 return fare).

National Express provides a nationwide coach service from this airport. Further information on travel and time schedules is obtainable from Heathrow Airport information desks in each terminal, and the London Transport 'Welcome to Britain Centre' in Heathrow Central Underground Station.

The car-hire companies Avis, Budget, Hertz and Europcar have desks in each terminal.

London Gatwick

This is the second major London airport and has recently been given a major facelift. Two terminals now serve over fifty different airlines. It handles a major cross-section of international scheduled flights as well as charters to overseas destinations.

Travel from Gatwick Airport. The airport lies to the south of London and the British Rail station is part of the South Terminal. The non-stop Gatwick Express runs every 15min during the day, and hourly at night, between the airport and Victoria Station in London. The journey takes 30min. There are also fast and frequent trains between Gatwick and mainline stations all over the country. The hourly train between Gatwick and the recently improved BR station at Reading opens up major rail services to destinations in the west and many other regions of Britain.

You will find the coach station on the ground floor of the South Terminal. Many of the coach services are similar to those described at Heathrow. For fuller information the visitor should contact the bus and coach information desks on the arrivals concourses in both North and South Terminals, which are open between 06.30 and 22.30.

The North Terminal and South Terminal are linked by a fast railway shuttle which runs every 3min.

Hertz, Avis, Europcar and Budget offer a full range of cars for hire and have desks at the airport.

Getting Information
Visitors who wish to make enquiries to international airports
in the UK for travel information, including flight enquires, will
find the telephone numbers set out below useful.

Aberdeen	0224 574281	Jersey	0534 22201
Belfast	0232 240522	Kingston	081 897 4000
Benbecula	0870 2310	Leeds	0532 446131
Birmingham	012 236 7000	London	071 987 4000
Bournemouth	0258 56621	London Gatwick	0293 518033
Bristol	0272 298181	Manchester	061 228 6311
Cardiff	0222 397071	Prestwick	0292 76836
Edinburgh	031 225 2525	Shetland	0950 60345/60224
Glasgow	041 332 9666	Stornoway	0851 3105
Guernsey	0481 24433	Wick	0955 3914

Domestic flights
There are well over a dozen airlines which provide a wide-
ranging domestic service. Some, as you can tell by their names,
aim specifically at providing a service from their regions to a
variety of UK airports (Jersey European Airways, Guernsey
Airlines, Manx Airlines etc). Other small independent airlines
(Brymon, Loganair, Air Écosse and Aurigny Air Services) also
offer services to targeted regions.

The largest airline working domestic routes, is, of course,
British Airways. It provides a Super Shuttle service between
London and Belfast, Edinburgh, Glasgow and Manchester with
a wide range of fares.

An Executive ticket enables you to turn up 10min prior to
departure, guarantees a back-up aircraft if the flight is full,
requires no reservation with payment and ticketing anytime
before travel, and gives a full refund on cancellations. These
tickets cost (single fare): Belfast £82, Edinburgh £87, Glasgow
£87 and Manchester £68, from London. After this ticket comes
a whole range of savers to fit your requirements. They are Time-
Saver, Budget Saver, UK Saver, Early Saver and Standby.

The British Airways *Super Shuttle Information and Timetable* booklet will provide you with the restrictive clauses, flight

times and local reservation offices. There are some thirty-five throughout the UK.

During the week there are six daily flights each way to and from Belfast, ten for Edinburgh, twelve for Glasgow and twelve for Manchester. All Super Shuttles provide food on board: breakfast, daytime snack, lunch, tea and dinner, according to flight times. All British Airways domestic services are non-smoking. Super Shuttle now carries 3.5 million people each year and is one of the biggest carriers of passengers in Europe, with some three thousand scheduled flights annually and several thousand unscheduled flights, resulting from BA honouring its pledge that every passenger will be able to travel on a flight of his or her choice.

At every Super Shuttle airport, Hertz Car Hire provides a range of vehicles which can be hired in the departure lounge prior to take-off. At Heathrow, Executive ticket passengers have access to the Rank Xerox Business Support Centre, with photocopying, fax and phone facilities.

In order to reduce check-in times, British Airways has introduced TimeSaver machines in its Super Shuttle lounges. They augment staff check-in counters and, provided you have one of the airline's family of cards – the Airplus or TimeSaver mark such as Blue Chip or Executive Club – you can check in any time up to 15min before take-off. The TimeSaver machines only take 40sec to process your ticket.

To give a sample of the domestic services which some of the other airlines provide, you will find that Air UK flies from London (Gatwick) to Glasgow, from London (Heathrow) to Humberside and Norwich, and from London (Stansted) to Aberdeen, Edinburgh, Guernsey, Glasgow and Jersey. British Midland Airways flies from London (Heathrow) to Belfast, Edinburgh, Glasgow, Leeds/Bradford, Liverpool and Teeside. Dan-Air flies from London (Gatwick) to Aberdeen, Belfast, Inverness, Jersey and Newcastle.

Bargains
The above airlines also have an inter-city network in the UK, and flights to European cities from a variety of different British airports. They also offer special savers and discounts. When booking domestic flights anywhere in the UK it is therefore

advisable to call into your local travel agent for fuller information, just as with international flights.

Visitors to Britain can find a number of bargains, especially on long-haul routes, and should make enquiries at the local British Airways Office or at any ABTA (Association of British Travel Agents) tour operator for information.

To give an example of the sort of service and deals that can be expected from Britain's national airline, we will take one of the furthest long-haul destinations, Australia, as an example.

There are eight local Austap Travel Agents or British Airways Sales Shops in Adelaide, Brisbane, Canberra, Hobart, Melbourne, Newcastle, Perth and Sydney, where visitors can begin their enquiries. Here you will find that the airline, which books over 250,000 holidays a year, can advise you on where to stay and what to see at a wide range of destinations. British Airways has been serving the great cities of Europe for over fifty years, and the visitor who flies BA to London and back will be given a return ticket from London to any one of nineteen European cities absolutely free. Furthermore, you can even fly free to one European city, make your own way to another, and fly back to London from there.

It is possible, when coming over for a long stay, to buy a package holiday at one of a wide choice of hotels in the UK, advertised in the airline brochure. This may be more economical than booking your hotel separately and will allow time to make your own arrangements for a long-term stay (see 'Accommodation', chapter 6).

Passengers have a choice of three categories of travel, beginning with Economy, which offers a choice of three-course meals and complimentary bar service. Next up is Club Europe or Club World (long-haul) which is popular with the business traveller. Here the seats are larger and are specially designed for added comfort, which can make all the difference on a long flight if you are a large person, say over 1m 77cm (5ft 10in) and 77kg (170lbs). In-flight service is also greatly enhanced, as is menu choice. There is a quality full-bottle wine service, as well as the free bar service. First Class is super-luxury, with reclining sleeper seats, yet more space, videos selected from a library of fifty and individually operated from a panel in the seat arm, vintage connoisseur wines, six-course haute cuisine meals, chauffeur-driven hire-car service as required, and so on.

Finally it should be mentioned, although everybody knows it, that British Airways is one of two airlines that offers time-saving supersonic flights to certain destinations aboard her Concorde aircraft. Altogether the airline has seven Concordes and forty Jumbo Jets in her fleet of two hundred aircraft, and annually carries approximately 25 million passengers on scheduled and charter flights.

The airline has an arrangement with Kenning Motor Group where you can hire a range of vehicles, from an Austin Mini up to a twelve-seater minibus. Costs vary according to vehicle size and there are thirty-one different types of vehicle to choose from. An information pack and maps are provided with each vehicle and mileage is free, except for petrol costs. Subject to having a valid driving licence in your country of residence, with a minimum of one year's experience, drivers between twenty-five and seventy-five years of age can hire a car in the UK. Under certain special circumstances, it is possible for the lower age limit to be reduced to eighteen years of age.

If you book a British Airways Car Hire Holiday in advance, certain extras are provided free. These include roof racks, and baby seats and harness. Subject to a minimal rental period of seven days it is possible, in some regions, to hire a Metro or Montego adapted for use by the disabled. Four- to six-berth campervans are also obtainable for reasonable charges. There are large discounts, which improve the longer you have the vehicle on hire.

Around four hundred and seventy aircraft are operated by other British airlines. Dan-Air operates both scheduled and charter flights with over fifty aircraft. British Midland and Air-UK are both major domestic airlines. They both operate a range of international and charter routes. Air Europe is a major charter operator which is now expanding its scheduled services into Europe. Virgin Atlantic, with some of the best trans-Atlantic buys, is expanding into other routes. Britannia Airways is one of the largest charter operators in the world, and flies from some sixteen airports to over eighty destinations in Europe and overseas. Working mostly for its associate tour company, Thomson Holidays, it has carried over six million passengers in one year. Other leading charter services are Monarch Airlines and Novair International.

The Inland Waterways, Ports, and the Channel Tunnel
Besides road, rail and air there is a fourth mode of transport, which reached its heyday in Britain in the eighteenth century: the inland waterways. The building of the 'cross' system of canals linked the Thames, Humber, Mersey and Severn estuaries and created routes for freight between many leading ports and towns throughout England and parts of Wales.

Originally there were some 6,440 navigable kilometres (4,000 miles) of waterway. In the nineteenth century much of this was destroyed by the railways, which bought up sections of canal in order to break up the system and get rid of competition. In the early 1950s the government almost decided to reduce the inland waterways to 1,130-odd kilometres (700 miles), but fortunately this never happened. Today over 3,220km (2,000 miles) of canal have been restored, and cruising along them has become a major leisure pastime.

On the canals you will see hundreds of old-fashioned narrowboats with a maximum length of 21m (70ft) and maximum beam of 2m (6ft 6in). This is the largest size that most canal locks can accommodate. On the rivers, the Norfolk Broads, and certain Scottish and Irish lochs as well as the Caledonian Canal, craft with a broader beam can be navigated because existing locks on the rivers are wider. Throughout the British Isles it is possible to hire self-drive craft for holidays. Canals continue to be restored and the latest to be reopened is the Kennet and Avon, linking the Thames at Reading via Newbury, Bath and Bristol, with the Severn.

British Waterways is responsible for hundreds of miles of inland waterways in England, Scotland and Wales, and general enquiries about canals and cruising are handled by the Information Centre at Melbury House, Melbury Terrace, London NW1 6JX (Tel: 071 262 6711).

The main inland waterways which still carry commercial traffic are the Manchester Ship Canal, some waterways in the North-East, the link from London to Birmingham, the lower Thames and the lower River Lee. In Scotland there is commercial traffic on the Caledonian Canal, linking the east and west coasts, and in Northern Ireland a small amount of commercial freight is carried on the Lower Bann Navigation.

Ports
There are eighty ports of commercial significance in the UK, as well as many small harbours which provide anchorage for cruisers and yachts. Ferry services to and from the Continent of Europe and Ireland cater for 25 million passengers a year, many of whom bring their cars over. The main ferry operators between these destinations, and their routes, are:

Brittany Ferries, which has Portsmouth–Caen, Portsmouth–St Malo, Poole–Cherbourg, Plymouth–Roscoff, Cork–Roscoff, and Plymouth–Santander services. The pride of the fleet is the new *Bretagne*, linking Spain and the UK direct. Its accommodation is on a par with that of a luxury cruise ship, despite the fact that it also has garaging for 600 cars.

P & O European Ferries has services between Portsmouth and Cherbourg, Portsmouth and Le Havre, Dover and Zeebrugge, and Felixstowe and Zeebrugge. It also has a service between Cainryan in Scotland and Larne in Northern Ireland.

SeaLink British Ferries has services between Newhaven and Dieppe, Folkstone and Boulogne, and Harwich and the Hook of Holland, as well as three services between Britain and Ireland, which are Stranraer–Larne, Fishguard–Rosslare, and Hollyhead–Dun Laoghaire. Of particular interest is the SeaLink MV *Orient-Express*, which can be booked in the UK and provides a car ferry and cruise ship service around the Mediterranean, calling at ports such as Athens, Venice, Istanbul, Kusadasi and Patmos.

Sally Ferries plies between Ramsgate and Dunkirk.

There is also a good selection of other European-owned ferries, which supply a service between different parts of the Continent of Europe, as well as hovercraft and jetfoil services.

If you are not a good sailor, it may be useful to know that Hoverspeed offers the fastest surface route between England

and France, with a 35min scheduled service between Dover and Calais. It also takes cars.

Besides cross-Channel services, there are many useful passenger and car ferry services between the mainland of Britain and nearby islands. British Channel Island Ferries and Condor Hydrofoil run services between the south coast of England, and Jersey and Guernsey. The Isle of Man Steam Packet Company runs ferry services between the west coast of England and the Isle of Man. Caledonian MacBrayne, with its thirty roll on/roll off ferries, offers access to some twenty-three islands off the west coast of Scotland.

SeaLink ferries, Red Funnel and Hovertravel offer easy services to the Isle of Wight from several departure points on the mainland, including Lymington, Southampton, Portsmouth, and Southsea. The shortest journey takes only 10min. There are sailings to all the inhabited islands off the mainland of Britain and, for further information on schedules and routes, interested parties are advised to contact their local High Street travel agent.

Travel Around London
London's famous red double-decker buses go almost everywhere in London and the best way of seeing the city is, without doubt, from the upper floor of a double-decker.

You will see bus-stop signs with the numbers of the buses which stop there written up. There are also bus signs with the word 'Request' on them. If you want a bus to stop here, you must hold up your hand. London buses are numbered and their destinations en route are displayed on the front above the driver.

There is an unwritten rule at bus-stops that you must join the queue, or line up, so that everyone gets on the bus in the order in which they joined the queue. It may seem slow but at least it is a fair system, and it gives the elderly a fighting chance of getting on board.

Unfortunately the London bus service can be erratic, due to heavy traffic, and sometimes a whole batch of buses with the same number will arrive at the stop in a convoy. This makes the Underground faster and more reliable, though not such an attractive way of getting around London.

Buses in London start running around 05.30 and finish around midnight. Timetables are posted at bus stops. Night buses travel through central London from 23.00 to 06.00. They have the letter 'N' before their number and their stops have blue and yellow route numbers. You can obtain a *Night Owl* leaflet giving timetables and a route map for night buses from any Travel Information Centre.

A number of buses provide excellent sightseeing tours of London. They include Discovering London, which is a whole-day tour of historic London, including such venues as the Royal Albert Hall, St Paul's Cathedral, the Tower of London and Westminster Abbey. The fares are approximately £30 for adults and £26 for under-seventeens, and the pick-up service covers nearly twenty London hotels (Tel: 071 930 2377).

Cityrama, which operates open-top blue buses, runs two-hour tours of main London sites. The buses depart every half-hour on a daily basis from Grosvenor Gardens, Trafalgar Square, Westminster Abbey and Russell Square. Tickets for adults cost £5, and for children £2.50 (Tel: 071 720 6663).

A Culture Bus runs on a regular basis throughout the day, with pick-up points at the Victoria and Albert Museum, Harrods, Madam Tussaud's, St Paul's and the Tate Gallery. Tickets are valid for 24 hours and you can get on and off as you like. Tickets for adults are £3.50 and, for under-fifteens, £2.00 (Tel: 0702 355711).

London Regional Transport also runs red double-decker buses from Piccadilly Circus, Speakers Corner, Baker Street and Victoria station. Full information on their tours can be got by telephoning 071 222 1234. Tickets cost £5 for adults and £3 for under-sixteens.

River and Canal Boat Services
There is a Water Bus Service on the canal between Little Venice or Camden Lock and the London Zoo. The boats between these venues take approximately two hours and run every hour from 10.00 to 20.00 during the summer. The nearest Underground station for Little Venice (Tel: 071 286 3428) is Warwick Avenue and for Camden Lock (Tel: 081 482 2550), is Camden Town. The canal trip costs approximately £4.50 for adults and £2.60 for children. Another narrowboat travelling the canal along

this route is called *Jason*. For more information telephone
071 286 3428.

Other boat trips include:

The **Tower of London** from Charing Cross Pier, Victoria
Embankment (Tel: 071 930 0970/1). Nearest Underground
station is Embankment. First trip 10.00, then every half-hour
until 1630 daily. Adults £1.50 single, £2.20 return. Children 75p
single, £1.10 return. The journey takes 25min.

The **Thames Barrier** from Westminster Pier, Victoria Embankment (Tel: 081 740 8263). Trips leave the pier at 10.00;
11.15; 11.45; 12.30; 13.30; and 14.45. From Thames Barrier
(built to protect London from flooding by the Thames) they leave
at 11.30; 12.45; 14.00; 15.00; and 16.15. Adults £2 single, £3.50
return; children £1 single, £2 return. The journey takes 1hr.

Hampton Court (sixteenth-century palace of Cardinal Wolsey
and Henry VIII) from Westminster Pier, Victoria Embankment (Tel: 071 930 4097). Nearest Underground station is
Westminster. Trips at 10.15; 10.30; 11.00; 12.00; and 12.30.
Last boat back, 17.00. Adults £5 single, £6 return. Children £3
single, £4 return. The journey time is 4/5hr. A boat also leaves
from Richmond Pier (Tel: 081 940 3505).

Greenwich, taking in the Cutty Sark, Royal Observatory
and Maritime Museum, from Tower Pier (Tel: 071 488 0344).
Nearest Underground is Tower Hill. Trips at 11.00 and then
every half-hour until 16.30. Last boat back, 17.00. Adults £1.70
single, £2.80 return. Children 75p single, £1.10 return.

There are a large number of scheduled river services,
both up-river and down-river. Basically, river services go from
Westminster Pier to Kew, Richmond and Hampton Court.
Down-river services go from Westminster and Charing Cross
Piers to the Tower of London, Greenwich and the Thames
Barrier. River service times of departure can be checked by
telephoning the London Tourist Board's recorded River Service
line (Tel: 071 730 4812).

Underground Trains
London Underground Ltd operates Underground trains on
408km (254 miles) of railway and serves 273 stations, with some

470 trains operating during the peak period or rush hour. Tube trains, as they are colloquially called, run every few minutes and every station has Underground maps enabling you to plan your route in advance. Different lines are shown in different colours so that it is easy to see where to change. You can obtain a pocket-size Underground route map and train timetable from a Travel Information Centre, and many diaries printed in England carry an Underground route map, too.

Underground trains start around 05.30 and the average time for last connections on weekdays is between 23.30 and 01.30. On Sundays most trains, with a few exceptions, finish around 23.15. In all cases it is advisable to check these train times, which are displayed in the tube station.

Travel Information Centres are located in the following Underground stations, and are open at the times listed: Euston 08.30–18.00 daily; Heathrow Central 08.30–18.00 daily; King's Cross 08.30–18.00 daily; Piccadilly Circus 08.30–18.00 daily; Charing Cross 08.30–18.00 Mon–Sat; Oxford Circus 08.30–18.00 Mon–Sat; St James's Park 08.30–18.00 Mon–Fri; Victoria 08.30–21.30 daily.

The Docklands Light Railway
With the development of the docklands, particularly as a residential area, the Docklands Light Railway has been built to assist travel. It is about 12km (7½ miles) long with sixteen stops. Construction and further plans are afoot to extend the line.

Good Deals
You can buy a special ticket which allows virtually unlimited travel on London Transport buses and Underground trains, called the Visitor Travelcard. The ticket is available for one, three, four or seven days and must be purchased before you leave home, as it is not obtainable in Britain.

A bargain ticket called a Travel Card for bus and Underground, which can be bought in London from Underground stations, enables the visitor to enjoy unlimited travel within the system. A photo card with passport-size photograph, obtainable from Underground stations, is necessary for use with Travel Cards (except for the one-day Travel Card).

Taxis and Minicabs

Radio taxis provide a 24-hr service and for this you can ring any of the following numbers: 071 286 0286; 071 272 0272; 071 272 3030; and 071 253 5000.

London taxis, which are as famous as London buses because of their traditional design, can be hailed as they travel along or be picked up at standard taxi ranks at mainline stations and airports. Altogether London has some 16,000 taxis, out of the 50,000 licensed to 'ply for hire' in Great Britain.

It is customary to tip a taxi driver approximately 10 per cent on top of his metered fare, which you can see from your back seat. Extra charges are also registered for baggage which you have not taken into the rear compartment. Provided your journey is within 9.6km (6 miles) of the centre of London, a taxi should take you where you want to go. Sometimes they will refuse if it is a long journey and you will have to negotiate a fare. You will also have to negotiate any fares over 9.6km. If you have any complaints about the taxi service, make a note of the cabby's number – which appears below the Fare Table – or alternatively note the number of the taxi, and ring the carriage office (Tel: 071 278 1744).

Minicabs, which are slightly cheaper than taxis on longer distances, can be obtained by telephoning certain reliable services such as Abbey Car Hire (071 727 2637) or Addison Lee (071 720 2161). You will find that many of your friends, and hotel concierges, can recommend reliable companies. If you are going out to an airport and don't want the hassle of trains or buses, or the expense of a taxi, the minicab is a good choice.

Helicopters

Sightseeing tours of London by helicopter can be arranged for 15min and 1hr durations. For more information on these tours and London Heliports, contact Battersea Heliport, Lombard Street, London SW11 (Tel: 071 228 3232).

10
Stately Homes, Seasonal Events and Places to Stay

The history of the British Isles has been turbulent, but because the land has been isolated by the sea from the continent of Europe, much of the wildlife and many of the historic places remained intact until fairly recently.

Then, as the population increased with the Industrial Revolution, cities began to spread outwards into the countryside to accommodate human beings, and the natural habitats of Britain's wildlife diminished and, in some places, disappeared. Observation, however, shows that nature is very resilient and has a special kind of self-protective intelligence which is demonstrated by adaptability. As human beings have encroached on and changed the face of the countryside, so many small animals and a wide range of plants have changed their habits or found new places to thrive and prosper, some of them quite surprising. In the big cities and sprawling industrial estates you will find many places where nature has got an active foothold.

There are no less than 101,250ha (250,000 acres) of derelict wasteland and abandoned factory sites in Britain, which have been quickly taken over by wild creatures and all kinds of plants. Hence our great cities, such as London, Edinburgh, Glasgow and York, reflect much of our former wildlife as well as our eventful history, just as do the castles which abound in Scotland and Wales, and the stately homes in England.

In the past few years awareness of the environment and the need to protect it has become more than just a fashionable pose. It is now a vital necessity and the British, as stately home visitors, nature lovers and gardeners par excellence, have taken the ecology movement to their hearts in an effort to preserve their heritage and their countryside.

Today, there are a number of organisations with dedicated staff who make great efforts, at considerable expense, to preserve this heritage. They include the National Trust, the

National Trust for Scotland, the National Gardens Scheme, the National Parks of Wales, English Heritage, and so on. These trusts make it possible for people to visit and enjoy places of great interest, where the drama of the nation's history has been enacted.

The National Trust

The largest private landowner and conservation society in Britain is the National Trust (NT). Wherever you go, you are close to land that is protected and maintained by the trust. This includes, for instance, 56,700ha (140,000 acres) of fell, dale, lake and forest in the Lake District alone; prehistoric Roman antiquities, downs and moorland, fens, farmland, woods and islands, nature reserves and lengths of inland waterways.

The NT produces a 300-page handbook for members and visitors, which contains information on the 250 historic buildings and 130 gardens which are under its care and open to visitors. This is a detailed catalogue of places to see which has been divided into sixteen regional sections, covering England, Wales and Northern Ireland (Scotland runs its own National Trust). In each section the properties are described, which makes it easier for the visitor to enjoy the enormous variety of countryside in the trust's care.

There are two editions of the handbook: the members' edition, available from the trust's headquarters at 36 Queen Anne's Gate, London SW1H 9AS (Tel: 071 222 9251); and a trade edition, which is on sale in National Trust shops, in bookshops and stationers all over the UK. It is also available through British Tourist Authority offices overseas.

People wishing to visit these interesting properties can either pay an entrance fee or become a member of the NT. Membership falls into several categories. There are twelve-month memberships, which are: individual, £19; for each additional member of the household at the same address, £10, and each receives an individual membership card; family group, £34, which gives single-card membership to one parent and free admission for both parents and their children under eighteen years. For young people under twenty-three who wish to join independently of their family, there is a concessionary rate of £7.50. In addition there are life memberships – individual £425 (£275 for senior citizens of sixty years and over) – where members receive lifetime privileges and their card also admits one guest. Joint life membership for husband and wife costs £500 (£350 for senior citizens) and each receives one card for personal admission. Benefactors who contribute £2,000 or more receive a card admitting themselves and one other to National Trust properties without charge. For up-to-date information on membership and benefits, write to PO Box 39, Bromley, Kent BR1 1NH (Tel: 081 464 1111). Visitors who are members of Commonwealth trusts are admitted free to NT properties provided they show their valid membership card.

In 1975 the American society, the Royal Oak Foundation, was established, with the full co-operation of the NT. More than fifteen thousand Americans across the United States belong, and enjoy the benefits of full trust membership except for voting rights. Through the interest and generosity of its members and friends, the Royal Oak Foundation has helped the NT with grants of over $1.5 million to buy new properties and improve existing ones.

American visitors might like to know that properties which have benefited from their generosity include Clouds Hill (Dorset); Hadrian's Wall (Northumberland), built by the Romans to keep out the rebellious Scots whom they were unable to conquer; Knole (Kent); Monk's House (East Sussex); Powis Castle and Clive Museum (Wales); Ingtham Mote (Kent) and several others.

The Royal Oak Foundation has single membership ranging from $40 annually to life membership of $750, and $1,000 for husband and wife. Membership also includes entrance to properties owned and administered by the National Trust for Scotland. The Royal Oak Foundation has active chapters in New York, San Francisco, St Louis, Boston, Chicago, Dallas, and Washington DC.

With so many interesting venues under the care of the NT it is not possible to give a comprehensive picture of what there is to see and visit in a limited space, so here we will just mention a few of the more unusual sites.

On the literary front, one place of interest would be **Wordsworth House** at Cockermouth where the poet was born. The **Beatrix Potter Gallery** at Hawkshead has a newly created exhibition showing a selection of original drawings used in her children's story books. Both of these are in Cumbria. In Dorset at Higher Bockhampton there is the small thatched cottage where the poet and novelist **Thomas Hardy** was born, and in nearby Somerset, at Nether Stowey, is **Coleridge Cottage** where the poet wrote 'The Ancient Mariner'.

Of religious and historical interest are the **Farne Islands** in Northumberland. St Cuthbert died on Inner Farne in AD687 and here a chapel was built to his memory in the fourteenth century and restored in the nineteenth. Nearby is **Lindisfarne Castle** which was built in 1550 to protect the Holy Island from attack. Down in Cornwall is **St Michael's Mount**, a spectacular fourteenth-century castle built on the site of a Benedictine chapel established by Edward the Confessor, King of England before Harold, who was killed in 1066 by William the Conqueror of Normandy.

Engineers and architects might like to see the great **Cornish beam engines** near Redruth, one with a cylinder 2.3m (7ft 6in) in diameter, which were used to pump water out of the tin mines from a depth of 610m (2000ft). The engines exemplify the use of high-pressure steam patented by the Cornish engineer Richard Trevithick in 1802. Talking of steam, there is the small stone cottage at Wylam in Northumberland where **George Stephenson**, the inventor of the first steam locomotive, was born. In the Lake District the beautiful steam yacht, the *Gondola*, first launched 130 years ago, has been renovated by the NT and can carry eighty-six passengers in opulently upholstered saloons for trips around Coniston Lake. In Wales you can see the elegant **suspension bridge** by Conwy Castle. This bridge replaced the ferry back in 1826. It was designed and built by the famous engineer, Thomas Telford.

Those interested in looking at beautiful paintings might like to visit **Petworth House** in Sussex, where there is an important collection of pictures by Turner and Van Dyck. It is also possible to stroll around Petworth Park, which was landscaped by Capability Brown.

The military historian will be interested in examining the **Old Battery** near the dangerous cliff rocks known as The Needles on the west coast of the Isle of Wight. Here a former Palmerstonian fort was built 76m (250ft) above sea level and a

61m (200ft) tunnel leads to a spectacular view of The Needles. Of exceptional scenic interest is the **Giant's Causeway** in Northern Ireland. The Giant's Causeway was so named because of a remarkable geological phenomenon whereby vast quantities of basalt have cooled into thousands of polygonal (three to nine-sided) columns. There are interpretative displays and an audio-visual theatre at the visitors' centre.

Besides looking after stately homes and historic sites, the NT has about two hundred holiday cottages in some of the most beautiful parts of England, Wales and Northern Ireland. In fact, the accommodation ranges from a spartan fell cottage to a luxury flat in an historic house. Full details are given in a 64-page illustrated booklet called *National Trust Holiday Cottages*, available from National Trust (Enterprises) Ltd, PO Box 101, Western Way, Melksham, Wiltshire.

National Trust for Scotland
North of the border, Scotland has its own trust. The National Trust for Scotland was formed in 1931, some twenty-five years after that founded in the south. Its aim is to assist in the preservation of Scotland's heritage of historical places and beautiful landscape.

In its care, 'for the benefit of the nation', are over a hundred properties, covering 4,050ha (10,000 acres). Together they comprise a rich variety of castles, stately homes, historic religious buildings, islands, mountains, coastline, waterfalls and historic battlefields. The trust provides an annual guide to its properties, which are listed under five areas – Highland; West; Grampian; Central and Tayside; and Lothian, Fife and Borders.

For a twelve-month period the cost of single membership is £15; family, which includes husband and wife and their children under eighteen years, £24.50; and juniors (under twenty-three) £6. Life membership costs £300 for husband and wife, including their children under eighteen years. Senior citizens may join at half the specified rates in the above categories.

The benefits which accrue to members include free admission to Scottish properties and to the properties belonging to the National Trust in England, Wales and Northern Ireland. A copy of the annual guide and a quarterly magazine, *Heritage Scotland*, are sent free. Priority bookings are given for holiday cottages, base camps, work camps, caravan parks and campsites. Each year the trust also arranges a fortnight's cruise for members, which visits not only places of interest in Scotland and her offshore isles but also places like the Faroe Islands, Iceland, Scandinavia, and other interesting locations in Europe.

Among the many trust properties which literary people will not wish to miss is the **Bachelors Club** in Tarbolton. In this seventeenth-century thatched house Robert Burns, the Scottish bard, and his friends formed a debating club. The club is famous for its Burns dinners, where the haggis is always addressed with solemnity.

In Ecclefechan just south-east of Locherbie, the visitor can see the arched house where **Thomas Carlyle** was born and where there is a collection of his manuscripts, letters and personal belongings.

Visitors who have the right to wear the kilt will want to visit the **Bannockburn** Heritage Centre, close to where King Robert the Bruce of Scotland vanquished the forces of King Edward II of England in 1314. The **Culloden** Visitors' Centre in Inverness tells the sadder story of the place where Bonnie Prince Charlie was defeated in 1746 by the English forces led by the Duke of Cumberland. Here, in the trust's care, are the **Graves of the Clans**, the **Well of the Dead,** the **Memorial Cairn** and the **Cumberland Stone**. Both visitors' centres provide excellent historical displays and films about the period, with versions in Gaelic, French, German and Italian.

Just north of Kircaldy lies the **Royal Palace of Falkland**, which was the country residence of the Stewart royal family. It is also where Mary Queen of Scots spent some of the happier moments of her tragic life, 'playing country girl in the woods and parks'.

Everyone with Scottish ancestry will want to see the most important site in the martial and political annals of Scotland – **Stirling Castle**. It stands proud on high ground overlooking the River Forth and guards the gateway to the Highlands. Here the National Trust for Scotland has entered into an agreement with the Scottish Development Department (Ancient Monuments) to manage the visitors' centre, with its excellent historic audio-visual display in many languages.

A number of fascinating Scottish islands are owned by the

trust. These include **St Kilda**, where the cliffs of Conachair, the highest in Britain, and the world's biggest gannetry are to be found; the **Isle of Arran**, where the golden eagle may occasionally be seen in the Goatfell range of mountains; the island of Staffa, the location of **Fingal's Cave**, 69m (227ft) long and 20m (66ft) high, which inspired Mendelssohn to write 'The Hebridian Overture'; and the island of Iona.

The Island of Iona is a former bulwark of Celtic and esoteric Christianity, brought to Iona by St Columba in AD563 from Ireland. The oldest surviving building is St Oran's Chapel, c1080, which has been restored. Not far from the restored cathedral stands the tenth-century, elaborately carved Celtic Cross of St Martin, and a little beyond are the ruins of a thirteenth-century nunnery. For centuries Iona was the burial-place of ancient Scottish kings and chieftains, who also often came here to settle their disputes and take oaths of fealty.

Lord Kenneth Clark, the great art historian who is the author of the book *Civilisation* which was serialised on BBC TV, wrote:

> I never come to Iona – and I used to come almost every year when I was young – without the feeling that "some God is in this place". It isn't as awe-inspiring as some of the other places – Delphi or Assisi. But Iona gives one, more than anywhere else I know, a sense of peace and inner freedom. What does it? The light which floods around on every side? The lie of the land which, coming after the solemn hills of Mull, seems strangely like Greece, like Delos, even? The combination of wine-dark sea, white sand and pink granite? Or is it the memory of those holy men, who for two centuries kept western civilisation alive?

Culzean Castle (pronounced Cullane) and country park contains the trust's most beautiful rooms, designed by Robert Adam. The most spectacular is the circular salon, which combines all the characteristics of eighteenth-century elegance with the wild untamed scenery of sea, sky and mountain outside the windows, where the breakers of the Firth of Clyde beat upon the rocks. The castle was given by the 5th Marquis of Ailsa and the 16th Earl of Cassillis to the National Trust for Scotland in 1945.

In the same year, in order to show the nation's gratitude to the supreme commander of the Allied forces in the last World War, the trust offered General Dwight Eisenhower a 'National Guest Apartment' in the castle for use during his lifetime. General Eisenhower, grateful for the honour, stayed there on four occasions with his entourage, once when he was president of the United States. Today his room, with another five bedrooms in the apartment, can be rented. Enquires about staying in the National Guest Apartment can be made to the administrator (Tel: 06556 274).

Staying in Stately Homes
Many historic houses are available both as private holiday accommodation and as incentive and conference venues.

Historic House Hotels
In 1980 a company called Historic House Hotels Limited was formed by conservationist Richard Broyd, with the aim of restoring neglected houses of architectural and historical importance and running them as first-class hotels which preserve the atmosphere of a stately home.

First to be restored, in almost NT style, was **Bodysgallen Hall** near the quaint old-fashioned beach resort of Llandudno in Wales. It soon became clear from all the awards that were heaped on the hotel – including the British Tourist Authority Award for the restoration of an historic building, the Prince of Wales Award for outstanding environmental improvement, the Wales Tourist Board award for services to tourism, the Queen's Award for Export Achievement (held jointly with the company's next development, Middlethorpe Hall), the VS Hideaway Report for the 'Country House Hotel of the Year' and the Europa Nostra Diploma of Merit – that the words written by Henry James '. . . of all the things the British have invented . . . the most perfect, the most characteristic . . . is the well-appointed, well-administered, well-filled country house', were well observed.

Bodysgallen stands in its own parkland on a hill and the seventeenth-century house is furnished in the style of the period, with many fine pictures. The large entrance hall and first-floor drawing room have splendid fireplaces where fires are lit in the winter, and the flames are reflected on the stone-mullioned windows. The beautiful oak panelling adds to the feeling of warmth. The house has nineteen rooms as well as nine cottages grouped around a secluded garden courtyard, and a fine herb garden.

Middlethorpe Hall stands in 10.5ha (26 acres) of parkland and formal gardens only just over a mile from the medieval city of York. Apart from the fine period furniture and pictures pertaining to the Queen Anne-style house, there is a walled garden, a lake and some beautiful specimen trees. The property has won as many awards as its sister hotel Bodysgallen, including the Automobile Association star for food. Middlethorpe's individually decorated bedrooms are popular with racegoers, because of the hotel's proximity to York racecourse, and with conference organisers, because of the estate's small self-contained conference centre.

Hartwell House is the latest historic house to be restored by the company. It is a Grade 1 listed mansion, built at various periods between the sixteenth and eighteenth centuries. Its most famous epoch was when it was leased to the exiled King Louis XVIII, who held his court there from 1809 to 1814, at which time he left for France to take up the throne. Set in 28ha (70 acres) of parkland, which include a formal garden, a lake and several historic eighteenth-century garden buildings, the house is only 3.2km (2 miles) from Aylesbury and one hour's drive from Heathrow Airport.

The hotel has some fifty bedrooms, which include several suites and several rooms with four-poster beds. The beautiful library is available as a meeting room and can take up to thirty-five people seated theatre-style. The cuisine, like that of the other sister mansions, is up to the gourmet standard that was expected by King Louis XVIII.

Conference Venues
Talking of living in rooms where royalty has stayed, another popular venue for conferences is **Brockett Hall**. Here there are thirty king-size doubles, and one of the rooms is called Queen Victoria's Room. This is where Her late Majesty insisted on sleeping during her frequent visits. Lord Melbourne's Room is named after the former prime minister.

The State Banqueting Hall has the largest suite of

Chippendale furniture in existence, as well as Francis Wheatley's ornate and beautifully painted ceiling. It was here that Lady Caroline Lamb introduced the controversial waltz into England. Brockett Hall was used as a meeting place by foreign ministers and many heads of state at a recent EC summit. Chevrolet brought over incentive groups in chartered 747s, which landed at Hatfield Executive Aviation Airfield on the edge of the estate.

The most historic convention centre of all in England is probably **Leeds Castle** in Kent. In AD857 a wooden fort was built on the site, which became the residence of the chief minister to the King of Kent, Ethelbert IV. The minister's name was Led. The village was named after him, and it is from this derivation that today we have Leeds Castle.

The stone castle was begun by the Normans in 1119, and owned by the feudal Baron de Crèvecoeurs whose family gave much assistance to William the Conqueror. In 1278 the castle passed into the hands of Edward I and his wife, and thus began 300 years of royal ownership. Henry VIII loved Leeds Castle and converted it into a royal palace.

Today the estate is owned by the Leeds Castle Foundation, given to the nation by the Honourable Lady Baillie. The ancient castle, with its drawbridge and ramparts, has been a meeting place for kings, queens and statesmen for nearly a thousand years and today still remains a protective residential meeting place for those who require high-level security. It has recently hosted every kind of conference, from peace talks to economic meetings of international bankers.

On the 202ha (500 acre) estate, sport and leisure facilities include a golf course, tennis courts, swimming pool and croquet lawn. The castle's own hot-air balloon takes visitors for trips above the beautiful Kent countryside.

The National Gardens Scheme

It is interesting to note that the possession of a garden was, until the middle of the nineteenth century, confined to the owners of big houses. Then a huge spate of house building began all over the country, particularly in the suburbs where many small houses were given their own plot of land. Over the years some of these gardens became a home for hard-pressed wildlife whose original habitat had disappeared from the countryside as a result of all this building.

Rudyard Kipling, one of England's famous poets, wrote

Our England is a garden
And such gardens are not made
By singing – "Oh how beautiful"
And sitting in the shade.

By deduction this means that the 2,000 private gardens in England and Wales which are open to visitors under the National Gardens Scheme Charitable Trust are kept up by a legion of gardeners who are prepared to toil in the sun.

This trust produces annually a publication listing all the gardens in the scheme, with dates and times when they are open and the cost of seeing them. The patron of the trust is Her Majesty Queen Elizabeth the Queen Mother, and among the royal gardens on display are Frogmore Gardens at Windsor 'by gracious permission of Her Majesty the Queen', as well as Sandringham House and gardens in Norfolk. The gardens of the Duke and Duchess of Gloucester at Barnwell Manor are also open to visitors on occasion. More information on the National Gardens Scheme Charitable Trust can be obtained from its headquarters at 57 Lower Belgrave Street, London SW1 (Tel 071 730 0359).

The Scilly Isles
It should be mentioned here that one remote part of Britain, the Scilly Isles, is famous for growing early flowers for the London market. The Scillys are an archipelago of about a hundred and fifty islands, islets and rocks which lie some 48km (30 miles) south-west of Cornwall, and their mild climate (mean winter temperature 8°C, and summer 14°C) makes flower growing the chief occupation of the inhabitants.

Tresco Abbey has outstanding sub-tropical gardens which are well worth travelling to see if you are interested in gardens. Many southern-hemisphere flora are grown there, amidst the remains of a Benedictine monastery. The gardens are only a few minutes' boat trip from St Martin's Hotel, which is designed as a cluster of cottages nestling discreetly in the hillside opposite the deep channel of Tean Sound. Twenty-four individually-designed

other state monuments such as Hampton Court Palace and the Tower of London, as well as reduced admission fees to certain historic properties in Wales and Scotland. Members receive a copy of the guide free of charge together with a map for planning expeditions, and a quarterly journal with the latest news of current activities.

The tour-planning guide divides the properties into a range of types, which include abbeys and ecclesiastical buildings, historic houses, industrial monuments, gardens, medieval castles, later fortifications, Roman remains such as Hadrian's Wall, and prehistoric monuments.

Some of the English Heritage properties can be very inspiring and romantic; for instance take Tintagel, which rests upon the cliffs of the wild and savage north Cornish coast. Early chroniclers and great poets have told us of the magic of this place where King Arthur, son of Uther Pendragon and Ygrayne, is said to have been born.

English Heritage also produces an imaginative and varied programme of exciting and interesting events that take place during the year at different properties. These include medieval combats with jousting, international longbow competitions, falconry and a Roman legionnaires parade. There are also concerts, which vary from jazz to classical music, from film scores to performances by the Royal Opera at Kenwood. From April to September there are over a hundred and twenty-five different events. These are open to the general public, but members often pay concessionary ticket rates. Fuller details of activities are to be found in the *Events Diary* produced each year. This, along with the guidebook and other information, is obtainable from the Marketing Division, Head Office of English Heritage, Keysign House, 429 Oxford Street, London W1.

Seasonal Events
Variety is the key to Britain's interesting heritage. Each county has its own special unique appeal and each season has its own events and its own special attraction.

Winter
Starting with winter, we have Christmas Day, which is very much a time for family reunions; and New Year's Eve, which

138

is a great time for party celebrations, particularly in Scotland whose bard Robert Burns immortalised the date with his poem 'Auld Lang Syne'. On New Year's Eve many people in London head for Trafalgar Square to see in the New Year.

The run-up to Christmas is filled with special events throughout Britain, which include carol concerts and nativity plays in churches and cathedrals. Brompton Oratory in London has great appeal for Catholics who wish to attend Midnight Mass on Christmas Eve. Everyone is hustling through the shops at Yuletide looking for presents, and many towns sparkle with fairy lights. In London, Oxford Street and Regent Street are particularly famous for their display. In Lincoln the Christmas Market matches some of the street markets in Europe, such as Munich.

Many people use this time of year to go on weekend breaks, staying at oak-beamed inns and hotels in the country. Your local travel agent in the UK will be able to recommend a whole range of special package holidays, which are arranged by tour operators at prices to suit all pockets. If you find yourself in a Scottish inn on 25 January, which is Robert Burns' birthday, you will no doubt be involved in the traditional supper of haggis, bashed neeps (turnips) and plenty of whisky – the national wine!

Many important activities connected with leisure and sport take place in winter, such as the London International Boat Show at Earl's Court, supported by other similar exhibitions throughout the country such as the Southampton and Birmingham boatshows. Important international exhibitions display the latest advances in motor engineering, showing the new cars that are appearing on the market; and if you prefer small-scale designs, the Alexandra Palace hosts a Model Engineering Exhibition. Among the many other major London exhibitions such events as the Crufts Dog Show and the Royal Smithfield Show should be mentioned.

In York, where there is a splendid Viking museum, visitors should try to attend the Jorvik Viking Festival. This celebrates the arrival of these invaders of ancient times, who had such a lasting effect on the life of these islands.

Rugby enthusiasts have several field-days at this time of year, with international matches taking place at Twickenham, Cardiff Arms Park and Murrayfield, as well as in Paris. Other international sporting events include the Olympia International Show Jumping Championships. Skiing has come into its own in Scotland particularly around Aviemore.

Spring

Spring is beautiful in England because of the immense variety of colourful flowers and shrubs which bloom – bluebells, primroses, daffodils, tulips, magnolia and cherry – to mention but a few. It is the best time of year to visit the gardens of many of the historic houses open to the public.

Horse-racing enthusiasts crowd the many race meetings, including point-to-points and steeplechases. Among the leading events are the Chelthenham Gold Cup, and the Grand National at Aintree. The Badminton Horse Trials take place in May. The soccer season comes to its climax with the Football Association Cup Final. River fishing, which attracts over three million anglers in the UK, is at its best in May. The freshwater trout season begins in March.

Summer

Summer is the time for that strangest of English sports, cricket. This is a game that is an enigma to everyone who is not a member of the British Commonwealth, and it is likely to remain so. It is played in whites (ie, the players are dressed from head to toe in white) on village greens throughout the country, and on famous cricket pitches such as Lords, the Oval and Old Trafford. The uninitiated might be forgiven for thinking that the whole thing is some sort of arcane rain-making ceremony, as one of the most common phrases heard in connection with the game is 'Rain stopped play'.

The more international game of golf is holding many championship matches at this time of year. Among the more famous venues is the Royal and Ancient Golf Club at St Andrews in Scotland, where it all began nearly two hundred and forty years ago on 14 May 1754. 'Twenty-two Noblemen and Gentlemen, being admirers of the ancient and beautiful exercise of the Golf' met to sponsor a silver club award, to be competed for on the Old Course. Since then the Old Course has staged the Open Championship twenty-two times and the Amateur Championship fourteen times. Many championship matches are held at other golf courses all over the British Isles, and these have an immense following.

Summer also sees the International Lawn Tennis Championships take place at Wimbledon, the International Rowing Championships at Henley Royal Regatta, the International TT Motorcycle Races on the Isle of Man, and several important motor-car rallies, including an international one organised by the Royal Scottish Automobile Club. Yachtsmen come from around the world to participate in Cowes week, with its 'Round the Island' and Fastnet races.

Music-lovers have a heyday with the Glyndebourne Festival Opera Season, the Aldeburgh Festival of Music and the Arts in June, the Cheltenham International Festival and St Albans Organ Festival in July and, in August, the Proms (see p147) and the Edinburgh Festival, probably the largest and most comprehensive arts festival in Europe. This festival is brought to a close with the famous Edinburgh Military Tattoo, a stirring ceremony which is now televised round the world.

Theatregoers, who have an all-year-round diary in Britain, see the start of many important events during this period. Many fine productions with first-rate dramatic performances by the Royal Shakespeare Theatre Company can be seen both in London at the Barbican Centre and at Stratford-upon-Avon. The Shakespeare season starts in June. The Chichester Festival Theatre also starts its summer season in June, and the Kings Lynn Festival of Music and the Arts takes place in June/July in and around this historic Norfolk town.

Autumn
In autumn, beautiful colours appear in the trees as the leaves change hue, and there is a slightly cold nip in the air. Churches throughout Britain celebrate harvest festivals, and fruit, flowers and wheatsheaves are used to decorate the aisles and altars in thanks for plentiful crops. In terms of events, we see a continuation of many of the summer programmes, as well as the beginning of more music festivals. It is also a time for those interested in equestrian activities, with the Horse of the Year Show at Wembley in London, and the start of the hunting season in October.

The Highland Games begin around this time. These include

'tossing the caber' (actually a treetrunk) and other strong-man events, combined with more gentle but equally enjoyable pastimes such as sword-dancing and the Highland Fling. The most famous event in Scotland is the Braemar Royal Highland Gathering, attended by the royal family.

In November there is Guy Fawkes Night, when there are firework displays throughout England commemorating the unsuccessful attempt to blow up the Houses of Parliament in 1605 with kegs of gunpowder. Guy Fawkes was held responsible and was 'terminated with extreme prejudice'. November is also the month for the Lord Mayor's Show, which makes its way through London with great pomp and circumstance, the new Lord Mayor of London riding in a golden coach.

Of enormous interest to motorcar buffs is the London to Brighton Veteran Car Run, which was immortalised in the film *Génévieve*. Here you see some of the earliest motoring machines known to man and – talking of old things, this is the season when the Chelsea Antiques Fair takes place.

Art and literature devotees are catered for by the Cheltenham Festival of Literature, and the Belfast Festival of Arts at Queens.

Scottish Opera has regular seasons in Aberdeen, Edinburgh, Glasgow, Liverpool and Newcastle-upon-Tyne between September and June. Telephone 041 248 4567 for information. The Welsh National Opera has regular seasons at its home in Cardiff as well as in theatres in Birmingham, Bristol, Oxford, Southampton and Swansea. More information from Cardiff, telephone 0222 464666.

It is impossible to do more than give a taste of the multifarious events which take place in the UK during the various seasons. There are a large number of functions which are not annual. It is worth getting a calendar of events, which is available from any of the official tourist bodies such as the British Tourist Authority, the English Tourist Board, the Wales Tourist Board, the Scottish Tourist Board and the Northern Ireland Tourist Board, in order to decide which activities you wish to attend.

Where to Stay
Students will find that one of the cheapest ways to see the country is by staying in youth hostels. These are run by the

Youth Hostels Association (YHA) for England and Wales. There are over two hundred and sixty hostels, some in towns and cities and others in rural settings. If you are a member of the YHA in your own country you get access to hostels worldwide. For full information contact the Youth Hostel Association, Trevelyan House, 8 St Stephen's Hill, St Alban's, Hertfordshire AL1 2DY (Tel: 0727 55215).

There is such a plethora of books and booklets on the subject of all types of holiday accommodation that the visitor is spoilt for choice. The Automobile Association's (AA) travel agencies carry a whole range and the AA produces some of its own. Its book on *Hotels and Restaurants in Britain* has a star-rating system. The hotel assessments are carried out by the AA's own inspectors and are therefore pretty reliable. Less expensive accommodation is listed in *AA Inspected Bed and Breakfast in Britain*, which gives details of where to stay in guesthouses, farms and inns.

Every tourist association produces its own literature. For example, there is the *British Tourist Association Commended – Country Houses, Guesthouses and Restaurants* and other literature. There is the English Tourist Board's *Where to Stay – Hotels and Guesthouses*, as well as its publications on *Self-Catering Holiday Houses*, on *Camping and Caravanning Parks*, also *Farmhouses,* and *Bed and Breakfast in Inns and Hostels.*

Regional tourist boards print many other publications. For example the Heart of England, Wales, and Thames and Chiltern Tourist Boards publish the *B & B Touring Map*, which pinpoints were such venues exist and gives much of the information in three languages, English, French and German. The Scottish Tourist Board also has publications, in particular *Scotland – Hotels and Guesthouses.*

Call in at any tourist information centre, tourist board or travel agency, and you will be inundated with publications and lists. At information centres in some of the more remote areas, the staff will book you into somewhere to stay at a price to suit your budget. Their fee for this service is minimal.

In the past few decades staying in hotels has been something that most families have found difficult to afford and the major chains, as opposed to the small resort hotel, have catered mainly for the business traveller or the wealthy tourist. Indications are that this is beginning to change, and many low-cost chains such as Travelodge, Sleep Inns, Ibis, Garden Court and Courtyard are now starting to provide bed and breakfast accommodation at competitive prices and offer a challenge to the more traditional outlets in this category.

What the chains are doing is to provide comfortable but basic accommodation at an acceptable standard. The cost-cutting factor that makes this possible is doing away with the frills, such as gourmet restaurants, swimming pools, large decorative lobbies etc, and building away from town centres. Many of these hotels now offer nightly room rates from £25 for one person to £30 for a couple, or family sharing one room. Budget hotel accommodation is the fastest-growing side of the tourist industry. For less than it would cost to stay in a luxury West End hotel, you can now opt for a 'town house' such as the Egerton House Hotel in Knightsbridge. This new trend provides a high standard of comfort and friendly service.

11
Around Britain – England and the Capital

Sources of Information
Before coming to the UK you will probably have obtained considerable information on places to visit from the British Tourist Authority (BTA). Further information, in the form of booklets and brochures, is available from the tourist boards of England, Scotland, Wales, Northern Ireland, the Isle of Man, Guernsey, and Jersey.

Some of these tourist boards also have a London office where visitors can call in and get information. The Scottish Tourist Board is in Cockspur Street, the Wales Tourist Board in Piccadilly, and the Northern Ireland Tourist Board in Berkeley Street. The BTA, which has responsibility for promoting Great Britain overseas, has its offices at the same address as the English Tourist Board and has the same telephone number (see Appendix 3).

Within the major tourist boards there is a further breakdown into regional tourist boards, which have even more detailed information and literature on their own specific areas. For instance, in England there are tourist boards for Cumbria, East Anglia, East Midlands, Heart of England, London, Northumbria, the North West, the South East, Southern, Isle of Wight, Thames and Chilterns, the West Country, and Yorkshire and Humberside. Their addresses are available from the English Tourist Board.

Similar regional tourist board addresses are held by other national tourist associations. Hence it is possible for the long-stay visitor going to any particular area to obtain a wealth of background information on things to do and see. The holidaymaker should also keep a weather-eye open for tourist information centres, which provide information on local attractions, opening times, special events and transport. In some areas these offices will help you find overnight accommodation. The readily identifiable 'i' symbol on local signposts makes these tourist information centres easy to find.

In this chapter the author will attempt to give the reader a taste of things to do and see in some of the major cities and places of historical interest, while at the same time advising the long-term visitor to make the most of the encyclopedic knowledge which is available not only from the various national and regional tourist boards but also from a variety of trusts, some of which we will mention.

London

The most important venue, that nearly all visitors see, if not first then certainly at some point during their visit, is London. If you are going to stay in London for any length of time it is essential to purchase an atlas and street index, so that you can find your way around. Probably the best publication for this purpose is the *A to Z London*. This provides over a hundred sectional maps of London and the suburbs, all of which are well indexed; information on London transport facilities, including a useful map of the Underground railway network; and a map of West End theatres and cinemas. Once you obtain a publication such as this you will have no difficulty in finding the address of a friend who has invited you out to dinner, if he or she resides in the Greater London area, and you will also be able to arrange to meet people at the place most convenient to all parties. This is important when you consider that London is 56km (35 miles) across in some places.

Whether you are based in London or just passing through, you will find that the British Travel Centre, only a 2min walk from Piccadilly Circus (12 Regent St, London SW1Y 4PG), brings under one roof the BTA, British Rail and American Express, to offer a comprehensive information and booking service. The visitor can book coach, rail, and air travel, reserve sightseeing tours, theatre tickets and accommodation, as well as change currency.

The centre is able to provide information on the whole of the UK in many languages, and there is an excellent bookshop with over eight hundred different maps and travel guides which will help you save time and money in making arrangements. There is also a shopping advisory service and gift shop. The centre is open seven days a week, Mon–Fri 09.00–18.30; Saturday and Sunday 10.00–16.00, with extended Saturday opening during mid-May–September. The telephone information service number is 071 730 3400, available Mon–Fri 09.00–18.30 and Saturday 10.00–16.00.

Entertainment Round-Up

The BTA produces a magazine called *London Planner*, which gives details of what is on in London each month.

All musical tastes are catered for in Britain. The best-known classical concerts are the Henry Wood Promenade Concerts (Proms), which attract young music-lovers who arrive on the night of the concert to 'promenade' – or rather, take a standing place (no booking) – at the concert in the Albert Hall. The Proms take place in July and August.

Jazz, rock and pop music details are given in weekly papers such as *Melody Maker* and *New Musical Express*. Pop concert tickets are usually sold by agencies (who will charge a small fee) or they can be purchased direct from the venue. If you are London-based then *Time Out*, and *What's On and Where to Go in London* will keep you up to date. There is also a telephone information service (0898 500696) for pop music fans, which will give recorded information on major pop concerts and festivals. In general, fans of rock, punk, heavy metal and pop will find their type of music and kindred spirits at the Rock Garden in Covent Garden, Dingwalls in Camden Lock, the Hippodrome in Charing Cross Road/Cranbourn Street, the Hammersmith Odeon, the Town and Country Club in Kentish Town, and the Wembley complex. The Camden Palace has giant video displays, laser lights and an audience who favour very original styles of dress.

Lovers of folk music should make contact with Cecil Sharp House, 2 Regent's Park Road, London NW1 7AY, and jazz fans will already have heard of the famous Ronnie Scott's Club in Soho. They should also look out for concerts at the 100 Club in Oxford Street, the Bass Clef at 35 Coronet Street, London N1, the Pizza Express restaurant in Dean Street, and the Pizza on the Park at 11 Knightsbridge.

The Royal Opera House, Covent Garden and the London

Coliseum (home of the English National Opera) in St Martin's Lane will need no introduction to those who love opera. The Royal Opera House operates a student standby scheme for cheaper tickets.

While classical musical concerts are given all over the country and more or less all year round, as we have detailed in the previous chapter, the best-known venues in London are the Royal Festival Hall, Queen Elizabeth Hall and the Purcell Room at the South Bank Centre, the Royal Albert Hall, St John's Smith Square (a lunchtime concert at a modest price every Monday), and the Barbican Hall in the Barbican Centre, home of the London Symphony Orchestra.

While London is obviously the mecca for those looking for nightlife, nearly all the major towns and cities have discos, dance halls and night clubs. Many of the clubs and discos are for members only but there is often a special membership available for visitors. For up-to-the-minute information consult *Time Out* or the BTA *London Restaurant Guide*.

Apart from the well-known West End theatres there are very good smaller theatres in London and all over the UK. Plays which eventually appear on the West End stage are sometimes given a run in the provinces beforehand, and these can be extremely good value. The national dailies, such as *The Times* and *The Guardian*, give details of what is showing on stage in London.

It is sometimes possible to buy tickets at reduced rates just before the performance begins. Check with the box office for standby tickets. Many theatres will only sell these special-price tickets to students and those London theatres which operate this scheme have an 'S' symbol in the theatre listings. Don't forget to bring your student identity card if you want to buy a Student Standby Ticket.

The Half-Price Ticket Booth in Leicester Square sometimes has tickets (for cash payment only) for selected shows, available on the day of the performance at half-price plus £1. This reduction is only available for tickets with a face value of £5 or more. The booth is open for matinee tickets Mon–Sat 12.00–14.00, and for evening performances it is open Mon–Sat 14.30–18.30.

While it is sometimes most convenient to buy theatre and concert tickets from a ticket agency, it is more economical to buy direct from the theatre or concert hall if possible. Always check first what the official box office price is, before purchasing from other outlets.

Fringe theatre is alive and well in Britain. All over the country there are 'theatre-pubs' and experimental theatre groups. In London there is the Cottesloe, which is part of the National Theatre, the Pit at the Barbican Centre, the Bush Theatre at Shepherd's Bush, the Young Vic in Waterloo and the Royal Court's Theatre Upstairs (Sloane Square). Fringe theatre has its own information centre and box office in London, situated in the foyer of the Duke of York Theatre in St Martin's Lane. It is open Mon–Sat 10.00–18.00 (Tel: 071 379 6002).

The younger visitor to the UK will find plenty to entertain him or her. It should be remembered, however, that people of under eighteen years of age are not allowed into pubs or drinking clubs.

Many galleries and entertainment centres are open in the evening. In London the Trocadero Centre at Piccadilly Circus is open from 10.00–20.00 and offers shops and cafés. Some exhibitions are cheaper in the evening, with reductions for students and young people. Always ask about reductions when booking cinema, theatre, and concert tickets. There are many matinee performances which enable you to meet friends afterwards and still manage to get home at a reasonable hour.

Many places have facilities for the young to meet, enjoy sports and games, and listen to music. Check with your local Young Men's Christian Association (YMCA) or youth club, who will tell you where you can meet young British people of your own age. These groups often have special evenings for particular activities, and you may find something to interest you and provide an opportunity to meet others with the same interest. You can get information about your nearest YMCA youth centre from the National Council of YMCAs, 640 Forest Road, London E17 (Tel: 081 520 5599). In London the Youth Centre behind the church of St Martin's-in-the-Fields arranges a wide variety of activities for young people. Telephone 071 930 2561 for more information.

In London The Fridge, Town Parade, Brixton (071 326 5100) has a monthly under-eighteens club night. The Empire Ballroom in Leicester Square does the same but not with a regular date. *Time Out* is a good source of information for nightlife, listing many under-eighteen discos.

Many local swimming baths, dance and fitness centres, badminton and tennis clubs have evening and daytime sessions. This sort of involvement is a good way to meet the British in a relaxed mood and to make the most of your stay.

Those interested in sport will find several outlets for their particular choice. You can ski on the numerous dry slopes around the country and if you contact the British Ski Federation, 118 Eaton Square, London SW1W 9AF (Tel: 071 235 8227/8) it will send you a list of dry slopes. You will need to send a stamped addressed envelope.

Ice-skating and roller-skating are very popular sports and you can get full information from the National Skating Association, 15-27 Gee Street, London EC1V 2RU.

London Landmarks

Trafalgar Square is, by tradition, the very heart of London and all distances from the city are measured from the statue of Charles I. This statue looks towards The Banqueting House, where the scaffold was erected for Charles I's execution in 1649.

Trafalgar Square itself was conceived by Nash and has been described as the finest site in Europe. It began as the eastward extension of Pall Mall and replaced the Royal Mews stables, including one pertinently called Dung Hill Mews.

When Lord Horatio Nelson finally obliterated Napoleon's navy at the Battle of Trafalgar in 1805, at the price of his own life, it was decided to erect a monument to him. His statue is mounted on a 52m-high (170ft) granite column. At the base are four splendid bronze lions, and the bronze reliefs on the podium depict the major battles which Nelson fought during the Napoleonic Wars. They are said to have been cast from French cannon.

In the square are two fountains, once used as swimming pools on nights of indecorous revelry, and at Christmas time there is a large Christmas tree, presented by Norway as a thank-you for the help given by the British in World War II when Norway was under Nazi rule. The square is often a rallying point for outdoor marches and meetings, and more often than not it may be used for this purpose on a Sunday afternoon. It is also a favourite place for photographing the family feeding pigeons.

On the north side of the square is the **National Gallery**. This contains one of the finest art collections in the world, with masterpieces of every school from the thirteenth to the nineteenth century. The collection was founded in 1824, when parliament voted to spend £60,000 on the purchase of thirty-eight paintings from the collection of a wealthy financier.

Just behind the gallery, in St Martin's Place, lies the **National Portrait Gallery**, founded in 1865. It houses a priceless collection of 10,000 portraits of people who played a part in the country's history. Nearby is Leicester Square, with a statue of William Shakespeare as the centrepiece and dominated on three sides by enormous cinemas.

At the north-east corner of Trafalgar Square you can walk north, and within a few yards you will come to Nurse Edith Cavell's statue and St Martin's Lane, which houses many of London's famous theatres.

Leave St Martin's-in-the-Fields on your left and walk due east and you will pass Charing Cross Station and reach the Strand. If, as you continue down the Strand, you turn left into Southampton Street, you will come to **Covent Garden**, which was originally laid out for the Duke of Bedford as London's first square by Inigo Jones. Influenced by the Italian style, it was first called 'The Piazza'. A fruit and vegetable market operated here for over three hundred years. The market was relocated in 1974 and now this attractive venue has become a shopping and entertainment precinct, and is well worth a visit.

Apsley House, Piccadilly, which was at one time the home of the Duke of Wellington and had the address Number One, London, contains the Wellington Museum and the Waterloo Gallery, with works by Flemish, Dutch and Italian masters. It was acquired by the nation in 1947 and opened to the public in 1952.

The Banqueting House, Whitehall, London W1, is a superb example of Palladian architecture built by Inigo Jones in 1619. It contains a ceiling painted by Rubens, commissioned by Charles II. Rubens received £3,000 and a knighthood for his efforts.

Buckingham Palace is the Queen's London residence, and you can tell when she is at home as then the royal standard is flown. The house was 'done over' for Queen Victoria, who was the first British monarch to live there.

The changing of the guard takes place at approximately 11.30 every day in summer, and every other day from the middle of August to early April, but not if it is raining or if there is another state occasion taking place on the day. The best place from which to get a good view of the proceedings is the Queen Victoria Memorial, or the centre gates of the palace. It is a very popular 'sight', so arrive about 1hr in advance if possible. The new guard forms up at Wellington Barracks and marches, headed by a military band, to the forecourt of the palace. Music is played in the forecourt of the palace.

The home of Queen Elizabeth the Queen Mother is **Clarence House** (built by Nash in 1825), halfway down the Mall. A piper plays in the garden every morning at 0900 when the Queen Mother is in residence, as a tribute to her Scottish ancestry. The present Queen Elizabeth II lived there until her accession in 1952.

Charles Dickens' House is 48 Doughty Street, London WC2. The great novelist and social commentator lived here while he was writing *Oliver Twist* and *Nicholas Nickleby*. It houses the world's most complete Dickens library, and has been arranged to look as it would have during the author's time there, with many personal relics.

Greenwich Observatory, Greenwich Park, is the home of the old Royal Observatory, founded by Charles II in 1675 and since moved to Sussex. The 24-hr clock outside shows Greenwich Mean Time. The Greenwich Meridian, marking the earth's prime meridian (00 longitude) crosses the courtyard. Here you will also find the **National Maritime Museum**, tracing Britain's history of sail and steamships, with relics of Lord Nelson and Captain Hook and models of the great clipper ships.

Ham House, Richmond, is a National Trust property which provides a picture of life in the seventeenth century. Many of its furnishings date from the 1670s, and there is an attractive formal garden of the period.

Hampton Court Palace was begun in 1514 by Thomas Wolsey, a butcher's son who rose in the ranks of the church to become a cardinal. When he fell out of favour in 1529 the palace passed to Henry VIII. The gardens were laid out by William III.

There is a collection of some five hundred paintings, including works by the Italian masters, acquired by Charles I from the Duke of Mantua.

Hogarth's House, by Great West Road, Chiswick, was the summer residence of William Hogarth, the famous eighteenth-century cartoonist, painter and illustrator, who was a man with a strong social conscience. During the last war it was bombed, and then renovated in 1951. It houses a collection of Hogarth's prints, and eighteenth-century furniture.

Dr Samuel Johnson's House in Gough Square has contemporary portraits, and visitors can view the attic where the 'great lexicographer' worked on the first English dictionary.

London Parks

London has more parks than any other city of its size in the world, and you will find that you are never too far from somewhere to sit and watch the world go by. One of the biggest London parks is **Hyde Park**, which together with **Kensington Gardens** covers 25ha (635 acres). In Norman times Hyde Park was a forest, where herds of wild animals roamed. From the conquest until the dissolution of the monasteries it belonged to the monks of Westminster Abbey. During Henry VIII's reign it became a deer park. Deer continued to graze here, together with cows and sheep, until the middle of the nineteenth century. In 1654 Cromwell shot himself in the leg here, although not intentionally. Hyde Park was once a popular place for duelling. Shelley's first wife, Harriet Westbrook, drowned herself in the Serpentine, the artificial lake of 16.6ha (41 acres) which stretches through Hyde Park and Kensington Gardens. In the summer the Serpentine is thronged with boats and bathers, and on Christmas Day some hardy spirits take a ritual swim in it.

Kensington Gardens are divided from Hyde Park by a roadway from Knightsbridge to Bayswater, and they once formed part of the garden of Kensington Palace. They were laid out mainly by Queen Caroline, wife of George II, in 1728-31, and have beautiful avenues of trees, fountains and ornamental birds. At the north end is Long Water, part of the Serpentine, and on the west bank Peter Pan, the hero of Sir

J. M. Barrie's famous story, is commemorated with a sculpture by Sir G. Frampton (1912).

St James's Park, by Buckingham Palace, was originally a piece of marshland that was drained by Henry VIII to create a deer-park. Charles II liked to exercise his dogs here and to swim in the lake. The pelicans are said to be descendants of those presented to King Charles by the Russian ambassador in 1665. The park was laid out in its present form by John Nash, the architect of the beautiful Carlton House Terrace.

Kew Gardens, which lie on the west side of London, are officially the Royal Botanic Gardens, covering 116.6ha (288 acres). They were established in 1759. Many magnificent trees were lost in a huge storm in 1987. Some of the original garden ornaments still to be seen include the orangery and the Chinese pagoda. The gardens display the English horticultural taste for mixing the homely and the exotic.

Battersea Park, just south of the Thames, was laid out in 1858. It has a boating lake, sub-tropical garden, and sculptures by Henry Moore. The Duke of Wellington fought a duel here in 1829. An annual Easter Parade is held in the park, as well as a circus during the summer.

Green Park, which lies adjacent to St James's Park, is a tree-studded grassland covering 21.5ha (53 acres). It was added to the royal parks by Charles II. The Queen's Walk was named for Queen Caroline, wife of George II. Charles II had ice-houses built here for the royal picnics.

Hampstead Heath is the highest point in London and covers 334ha (825 acres). Constable used it as a subject in many of his paintings.

Holland Park, near Notting Hill Gate, is a well-wooded park with peacocks, an orangery, adventure playground and open-air theatre.

Regent's Park and **Queen Mary's Gardens**, with Primrose Hill, cover 191ha (472 acres). The park was originally a royal hunting ground and was laid out in its present form by John Nash in 1812. It also contains **Regent's Park Zoo**. Queen Mary's Gardens form a circle covering 7.3ha (18 acres). They contain a magnificent rose garden, lily pond, and fountain sculpture by McMillan (1950). The famous open-air theatre holds performances of Shakespeare's plays in summer.

Galleries
London's art galleries and museums are justly famous, and entrance to most of them is free. At the **Royal Academy** in Piccadilly the Summer Exhibition is held annually from May to July. The **Barbican Art Gallery**, London Wall, London EC2, has touring as well as its own exhibitions. Over on the South Bank is the **Hayward Gallery**, which houses touring exhibitions.

The **Tate Gallery**, Millbank, London SW1, contains a permanent exhibition of British painting from the sixteenth century. It also houses the Blake and Turner collections, which are excellent, as well as modern paintings and sculpture, with works by the Impressionists, Surrealists, and the Pop movement. The sculpture includes works by Giacometti and Henry Moore.

The **Wallace Collection**: Hertford House, Manchester Square, London W1, is a magnificent eighteenth-century town house and contains London's finest collection of eighteenth-century French painting, as well as a priceless collection of furniture, sculpture, and porcelain. There is also an early self-portrait of Rembrandt.

The **Queen's Gallery,** Buckingham Palace Road, was built from the bombed ruins of the palace chapel. It has a changing exhibition of treasures from the royal collection.

The **British Museum**, Great Russell Street, is one of the largest museums in the world, with numerous artefacts from ancient civilisations. The exhibits include the Rosetta Stone, which allowed scholars to interpret Egyptian hieroglyphic writing, the famous Elgin Marbles from the Acropolis in Athens, and sculpture from the T'ang dynasty in China.

Within walking distance of each other in South Kensington are the **Geological Museum, Natural History Museum, Science Museum** and **Victoria and Albert Museum**.

The **Geological Museum** has a magnificent display of gems, including the Koh-i-noor diamond, and an audio-visual display on evolution, with a very dramatic earthquake. The **Natural History Museum** has departments dealing with zoology, palaeontology, mineralogy and botany, each with its own library and students' room. There are lectures and film shows on some weekdays (Tel: 071 589 6323 for information).

The **Science Museum**, which also houses the **Wellcome**

Museum and the **History of Medicine**, has exhibits relating to every notable scientific discovery, including a comprehensive collection of machines, industrial plant and scientific instruments, with working models and examples of original and historic apparatus. Special film shows take place daily.

The **Victoria and Albert Museum**, which has lectures during the week (Tel: 071 589 6371), was founded in 1857 and is the national museum of applied arts. It covers an area of over 4.8ha (12 acres). The Primary Galleries show examples of all the arts, brought together by style, period and nationality, with a set of complete rooms and decorative suites from four centuries. The Study Collection contains exhibits grouped within the various classes: ceramics, sculpture, textiles, furniture, prints and woodwork. The **Boilerhouse Project**, in the basement of the Henry Cole Wing, houses a permanent collection about industrial design, and temporary exhibitions of modern design.

Sir John Soane's Museum, by the Law Courts in Lincoln's Inn Fields, London WC2, is in the former home of Sir John Soane, architect of the Bank of England. His collection of antiquities and works of art includes eight paintings by Sir William Hogarth entitled 'The Rake's Progress', as well as the sarcophagus of Seti 1. Every inch of available space is ingeniously used, and there are walls on hinges which swing back to reveal paintings.

London Shopping
Whether you have 'loads-a-money' or just want to browse hoping to spot a bargain, London is the place. The serious shopping takes place in the Oxford Street/Regent Street/Bond Street area. Most department stores are open from 09.00 to 17.30 but some stay open until 19.00 on Thursdays, and in Knightsbridge and High Street Kensington until 19.00 on Wednesdays. In Covent Garden Market shops open at 10.00 and close at 20.00.

Oxford and Cambridge
The two great university cities of Oxford and Cambridge are just over one hour's drive from London, but in different directions. In both of them you will find architectural gems

among the many colleges: there are thirty-five colleges in Oxford and twenty-five in Cambridge. At Oxford the oldest colleges, which were endowed as separate bodies with their own rules and privileges, are Balliol (founded before 1266), Merton (1264) and University (1249). The oldest at Cambridge is Peterhouse (1281).

The crowning glory of architecture in Cambridge is King's College Chapel, which was the centrepiece of King Henry VI's plan for his foundation. Equally famous is the King's College Choir, which sings at all the services – on Christmas Eve the service of nine lessons and carols is broadcast by radio and televised. Of great architectural interest in Oxford is Christ Church, which houses the smallest cathedral in England, predominantly late Norman in appearance (rebuilt 1141-80). The college's famous cupola-topped Tom Tower, which was designed by Wren in 1681, contains a huge 6.35 tonne (6.25 ton) bell taken from Osney Abbey. Every evening at 21.05 the bell rings 101 times, as it did in olden times when it used to summon the 101 undergraduates of the original foundation back to college as the gates closed for the night.

There is so much architecture and history attached to these two universities, which in recent times have seen the Prince of Wales (Cambridge) and the present Prime Minister Margaret Thatcher (Oxford) as undergraduates, that both universities warrant at least a full day's sightseeing. For those who would like to see these famous rowing universities from the river, punts can always be hired during the summer. Incidentally, Cambridge undergraduates punt from the platform and Oxford undergraduates from the other end.

Canterbury and York
In England there are only two archbishoprics, one of York and the other of Canterbury. The city of York is the archiepiscopal see of the Archbishop of York, who bears the title of Primate of England, and his sway extends over fourteen dioceses in the north Midlands and the north of England.

York
York is famous for its narrow streets, medieval walls and stately Minster. It ranks among the ten most visited destinations in

the world, relative to the size of its population. History reveals that the first emperor to visit York was Hadrian, who built his famous wall to keep out the fearsome Scots. Constantine the Great was proclaimed emperor here.

One quarter of all the medieval stained glass in England is housed in York Minster, which is the largest cathedral in England of its period. The tradition of this glasswork has been greatly enhanced by the remarkable restoration of the Rose Window, following a fire. The window was recently rededicated in the presence of the Queen.

Actually the cathedral, like the Firth of Forth Bridge, is always having some part of its structure restored. There is a saying in York that if the scaffolding is ever completely removed, the Catholic church will claim the Minster back.

Many of the narrow streets are called after their historic trades, such as Colliergate, where coal merchants forgathered, and Spurriergate, home of the spurmakers. Some of the overhanging houses in these alleyways are so close that neighbours were able to whisper gossip and criticise each other's work without being overheard in the street below. *Tristam Shandy* was published by John Hinxman 'at the sign of the Bible' in Stonegate.

If you want to know more of the goings-on in olden times, there are organised ghost walks which will take you through these eerie snickerways.

Among the top ten attractions of England is the recently expanded Jorvik Centre, where the visitor can journey in an electric car through a rebuilt Viking community. It is like going back a thousand years and experiencing not only the audible and visual aspects of a bygone age, but also the pervasive smell of musty hay, fish wharves and smoke. It is very realistic and much of the knowledge that went into the construction of this venue was obtained from a local dig, which exposed the largest Viking remains outside Scandinavia.

Among the numerous interesting places to see is **Castle Howard**, visited by Queen Victoria and recently popularised in the film *Brideshead Revisited.*

The **National Railway Museum** houses the fast steam locomotive *Mallard* (202.7kmph/126mph). **Bar Convent**, York's newest museum, is devoted to the history of Christianity and houses the withered hand of Margaret Clitherow, who in 1970 was canonised St Margaret of York. She was pressed to death by heavy stones for sheltering Jesuit priests in 1586.

There are two stately houses in York which demand attention for their display of historical furniture and excellent restoration. Overlooking York racecourse is the William III country house whose restoration has been carried out by Historic House Hotels to make **Middlethorpe House Hotel**, one of the most elegant places to stay in England (see p137). The ambience of fine English country house living is brought to perfection by the warmth of the hospitality and the imaginative cuisine, as much as by the restoration and furniture.

The other recently restored house in this area is **Fairfax House**. The work was carried out by the York Civic Trust under the patronage of HRH the Duchess of York. The interior offers a fine display of Georgian furniture. Although on the map York appears to be some distance from London (326.7km/203 miles), there are plenty of trains each day and it can be reached from the capital in under two hours.

Canterbury

Canterbury, which is just south of London, is the archiepiscopal see of the Primate of All England. Its splendid cathedral rests by the river Stour amid a scene of peaceful meadows, orchards and hop-gardens. The present building was begun by William the Conqueror's first Norman archbishop, Lanfranc, in 1070 and was erected on the ruins of an Augustinian church which burned down one year after the Norman invasion. It was completed in 1503 and, although Canterbury ranks only as the ninth largest of the English cathedrals, her majestic proportions and extraordinary history place her among the leading cathedrals of the world.

It was the famous words of Henry II, 'Who will rid me of this turbulent priest?' that led to the murder of the archbishop Thomas à Becket in the cathedral in 1170. His canonisation two years later drew pilgrims to Canterbury from all over England, and many parts of the Continent. Among them was Louis VII of France, who came in 1179. Chaucer speaks much about these pilgrimages in his *Canterbury Tales*.

The city of Canterbury was bombed by the Axis powers in

1942 and much of the centre was destroyed. A great deal of it was unimaginatively rebuilt in the 1950s. However, the bombing did unearth the foundations of a Roman theatre, which is a great rarity in England.

Despite the postwar restoration, Canterbury still retains a market-town atmosphere, which dates back to the Roman era. Mercery Lane, the usual pilgrims' approach to the cathedral, was formerly lined with stalls and shops selling 'ampulles' of healing water from Becket's well in the crypt and medallions of the saint. The Lane leads from the High Street to the Butter Market.

At first sight the cathedral dominates the city but in actual fact it is only the most conspicuous of many buildings, domestic and ecclesiastical, that are worth visiting, and which reflect the continuing status of Canterbury in the Middle Ages, and onwards to the present day.

Besides the cathedrals of York Minster and Canterbury, there are those of Bristol, Chester, Chichester, Coventry, Durham, Ely, Exeter, Gloucester, Hereford, Lichfield, Lincoln, Liverpool, Norwich, Peterborough, Ripon, Rochester, St Albans, Salisbury, Truro, Wells, Winchester, Windsor, Worcester and Beverley Minster.

If you are planning to stay some time in England, and wish to see as much as you can, you will find it worthwhile getting in touch with the regional tourist boards of the areas which interest you. This will enable you to obtain more detailed information, so that you can plan to spend your visiting time as pleasurably and usefully as possible.

Berkshire

It is not possible in this book to talk about all the wonderful counties to see in England. Like the rest of the UK, England has a very rich heritage. The author has chosen Berkshire as just one example of the fascinating counties to see, on the grounds of its closeness to London, the venue where perhaps most long-term visitors are likely to stay or be sometime during their sojourn.

Windsor, a colourful town dominated by its historic castle, is only half an hour's drive from the outskirts of London. Windsor Castle is the largest inhabited castle in the world and has been the seat of British sovereigns for centuries. The state apartments are in use on a regular basis and contain many treasures from the royal collection, including the exhibition of Old Master Drawings, the exhibition of the Queen's presents, the royal carriages, and Queen Mary's doll's house.

Highclere Castle is another magnificent Berkshire fortification and has recently opened its doors to the public. On display are the Tutankhamun treasures which were brought back from the Valley of the Kings in Eygpt by the 5th Earl of Carnarvon, and rediscovered much later by the butler.

The Thames, England's greatest river and source of inspiration to many writers and artists, makes its peaceful way through the royal county, and its leafy banks and still water provide a perfect setting for picturesque villages like Sonning and Streatley. Kenneth Grahame lived in the boating village of Pangbourne, and it was there that he created the famous riverside tale of *The Wind in the Willows*.

Reading, the county town of Berkshire, bestrides the Thames almost in the centre of the county. This university town, with its own museum and art gallery, is a blend of old and new and has one of the best shopping centres in the south of England. Its excellent rail and road connections make it an ideal centre from which to explore. In the heart of the town are the Abbey ruins, parks and gardens, and the Kennet and Avon canal, which joins the Thames at Reading.

The west of the county has a proud heritage and pastoral scenes to rival any Constable landscape. **Newbury** is a busy market town with a romantic past linking it to two Civil War battles between Parliamentarians, or Roundheads, and Royalists. During the coaching era Newbury was a main stop-over on the London to Bath run. The history of the area is well presented in the former Jacobean Cloth Hall and eighteenth-century Granary, now transformed into a canalside museum. An annual event to be noted is the Newbury Spring Festival of music and art.

Nearby **Hungerford** is a charming town renowned for its antique shops, as well as its custom of electing the Court Leet in a colourful Hocktide ceremony which takes place on the second Tuesday after Easter. Two 'Tuttimen' and the 'Orange

Scrambler' have the enviable task of visiting houses with common rights to collect pennies from the men and a kiss from the women, in return for oranges.

The **Kennet and Avon Canal** makes its way through valleys and watermeadows to Hungerford and provides sport, fresh trout, and boat trips in traditional canal craft, or even in a horsedrawn barge in the summer. The canal accompanies the rivers Kennet and Avon through towns and villages, and runs all the way from the Avon at Bristol to the Thames at Reading. It has been restored in recent years, opening up forgotten views and vistas.

Berkshire has much to offer, with racecourses at Newbury, Ascot and Windsor, as well as historic houses, a safari park, and day cruises on the Thames. For further information on the county contact Shire Hall, Shinfield Park, Reading, RG2 9XD (Tel: 0734 875444, extension 3056, or 0734 876195 for the 24hr answering service).

12
Around Britain – Scotland, Wales, and Northern Ireland

Scotland

Since the union of the two Parliaments in 1707, Scotland has been constitutionally part of Great Britain, yet in many people's minds it still remains a separate country in its own right. This feeling is strengthened by the fact that the country has its own educational, legal and ecclesiastical systems. The Scots like to emphasise their nationality by producing stamps with a lion on them, and they issue their own pound notes. However, they are very cosmopolitan when it comes to making up and selling kilts to visitors. Shoppers will encounter little difficulty in finding their name, regardless of what it happens to be, on a list telling them to which clan they belong and therefore which tartan they should buy and wear.

Edinburgh

The country's capital is Edinburgh. The city has a sort of wild beauty which makes it a brilliant setting for such annual events as the Edinburgh Military Tattoo, watched by a live audience of some four hundred thousand people through television, and the Edinburgh International Festival of Music and Drama, which is the most comprehensive arts festival in the world. Almost equally popular is the Royal Highland Show, which draws visitors into the capital for a four-day period. The showground extends over 37.6ha (93 acres) of the nearby 121.5ha (300 acre) estate owned by the Royal Highland and Agricultural Society of Scotland, which also attracts other major international exhibitions throughout the year.

Edinburgh Castle, which is perched like an eagle above the city, overlooks famous Princes Street and the enormous Gothic spire which forms a canopy on the monument to the author Sir Walter Scott. In niches of this edifice are historic figures and characters taken from Scott's 'Waverley' novels. Close by is Waverley Station. Above this is the great Clock Tower of the North British Hotel, which is always set four minutes fast to give the tardy traveller the hope of catching his train. The oldest part of the castle contains the saintly Queen Margaret's eleventh-century chapel, and the Old Palace houses the regalia of Scotland. It was here that Scotland's most tragic figure, Mary Queen of Scots, gave birth in 1566 to James VI of Scotland, who became James I of England. The ceiling carries his carved initials. Two military museums are also housed in the castle, which is open to the public from April to September 09.30–17.05 during the week, and 11.00–17.05 on Sundays; and from October to March, 09.30–16.00 during the week and 12.30–15.35 on Sundays.

Glasgow

Just one hour's drive due west of Edinburgh lies Glasgow, the commercial capital of Scotland, which is probably the most go-ahead conference centre in Britain as well as being the home of the Scottish Opera and the Scottish National Orchestra.

Glasgow has an impressive history, being an 800-year-old city, which in 1990 was nominated the Cultural Capital of Europe. Its buildings are deemed to have made the city the finest example of Victorian architecture in Europe. The architectural apogee is the City Chambers, which dominate the east side of George Square. Built in 1883–1888 and extended by John Watson in the 1920s, this imposing structure, with its 65.8m-high (216ft) tower, is built in Italian Renaissance style. The rich use of marble makes the interior as magnificent as the exterior. Two staircases rise from the loggia, which is built to the plan of a Roman Renaissance church. One staircase leads to the richly panelled Council Chamber and the other to reception rooms and the Banqueting Hall, with murals depicting the city's growth.

The same year as this building was completed, 1888, Glasgow staged the first of four international exhibitions, following Queen Victoria's Jubilee. It was visited by 6 million people. In 1901 the International Exhibition was the largest ever to be held in Britain, and featured art, industry and science. It was visited by 11.5 million people. This was followed by the Scottish

Exhibition of Natural History, Art and Industry in 1911, and the Empire Exhibition in 1938.

Just prior to their city becoming the cultural capital of Europe, the innovative citizens of Glasgow staged a Garden Festival right beside the Clyde. This drew visitors from all over the world. It was on the river Clyde that the once-famous shipyards built the majestic 'Queens' liners in the days when the words 'Clyde-built' constituted the supreme accolade.

Nowadays, with the demise of the shipyards, salmon have come back to the river; and downstream, the Clyde opens into the Firth of Clyde, one of the greatest yachting areas of the world, where the wind and light can change by the minute among the scatter of sea lochs and islands. And only half an hour from the city lie the 'Bonnie Banks of Loch Lomond', immortalised in Scotland's proudest ballad.

The city has two universities and it was here that one of her most famous sons, James Watt, perfected his discoveries of steam power. Next in importance to steam power, Scotland's greatest invention was probably the game of golf. This is still played all over the country at very reasonable prices, compared with the costs elsewhere. The home of golf is St Andrews, where nearly two thousand and forty years ago 'Twenty-two Noblemen and Gentlemen, being admirers of the ancient and beautiful exercise of the Golf' met to sponsor a silver club award to be competed for on the Old Course. This led to the founding of a club that, eighty years later, was granted by William IV the title of 'Royal and Ancient'. It became the governing body of the game and remains so to this day. Since then the Old Course has staged the Open Championship twenty-two times, the Amateur fourteen, and the Walker Cup eight times. Other great centres for golf are Turnberry, with the Arran and Ailsa Championship courses, and Gleneagles with the King's, the Queen's, the Prince's and Glendevon.

The Highlands and Islands
Some people say that the Scots also invented the Loch Ness monster. Others are convinced that this famous underwater resident actually lives in the loch, which lies close to Inverness, the capital of the Highlands. The place to start to try to discover whether the monster is fact or fiction, imagination or reality,

is the Official Loch Ness Monster Exhibition Centre in the pretty lochside village of Drumnadrochit. The centre, official headquarters of the Loch Ness National Archives, is the top attraction in the Scottish Highlands. A quarter of a million visitors come here every year to determine through galleries of pictures, storyboards, videos and exhibits, whether Nessie actually exists.

Since the 1930s there have been reported sightings by thousands of people, including members of parliament, policemen, AA patrolmen, farmers, tourists, gamekeepers, boat crews, and scientists. And there was one big-game hunter who found giant footprints on the rocky shore. Unfortunately his dreams of being interviewed on 'The 9 o'clock News' were shattered when it was discovered that the imprints had been made with a hippopotamus-foot umbrella stand.

The Highlands are a natural venue for all sporting activities which attract the visitor and his family – golf, tennis, angling, riding, rock climbing, skiing, sailing, and loch and river cruising – and let us not forget the Highland Games. Yet the region still has a lot more to offer besides.

'Caledonia stern and wild' was how Sir Walter Scott referred to his native country, a description which evokes a vivid image of the Highlands, remote and beautiful.

Throughout the Highlands and Islands people still continue to live in relative isolation, with on average only one person per 259ha (1sq mile). But, thanks to modern transport, we can now travel from one end of the British Isles to the other in a few hours, so the Highlands have become completely accessible to those who love what is beautiful and who value individuality and tradition. Highland customs continue to be observed and a knowledge of local traditions will add to the pleasure of a visit here.

It is interesting to note that people were living in the south of England for thousands of years before the first settlers we know of ventured into the Highlands. The reason for the time-lag was that a succession of Ice Ages sealed off the north of the British Isles while they were still physically part of the Continent of Europe. Eventually the sea managed to encroach, until finally it broke through to form the English Channel. The first people to leave substantial evidence of a settled existence in this region were the Neolithic farmers. They appeared about 4000BC and soon afterwards began to build varied and numerous chambered tombs – an architectural form seen today at its most spectacular at Maes Howe in Orkney.

The Highlands and Islands cover some 3.6 million ha (14,000sq miles) of territory lying between Shetland and the Firth of Clyde, an area of great fascination to those who are interested in the forces which shape our planet, since this is the most freshly minted landscape in north-west Europe. The landforms of this region have provided scientists with the evidence upon which to build theories which are applicable to areas beyond Scotland. But to many visitors the pleasure of simply walking over the landforms, and discovering the more remote parts, is all the satisfaction they require.

From the unspoiled character of this landscape we get some of nature's most spectacular displays of flora. Fragile alpines, sturdy oaks, and in places even plants whose natural homes are in warmer climes. For instance on the coast near the foot of Loch Maree are the Inverewe Gardens, now owned by the National Trust for Scotland, with a marvellous collection of tropical and sub-tropical plants. Osgood Mackenzie, who founded the gardens, described how in the mid-1800s peaches ripened on the walls at Canon House near Dingwall and colonies of wild bees in Wester Ross produced great quantities of honey.

The Highlands are one of the greatest reservoirs of wildlife left in Britain, home to the pine-marten, the wildcat, the polecat, the otter, the red and roe deer, red squirrel, and grey seal. You may even be lucky enough to see a fox climbing a tree, which he will do from choice or necessity, climbing up a vertical trunk to a branch as high as his weight can bear.

The Scottish wildcat is all the cat he ever was, as strong and robust as his prehistoric ancestors. Any big cat seen on the hill after dark, or caught in the car headlights on a Highland road, is more likely to be a true wildcat than a domestic moggie.

Birdlife abounds in the Highlands. The golden eagle, osprey and snowy owl are the best-known rarities. Dotterel, ptarmigan, and snow bunting nest on the high mountains. Crossbills, crested tits and capercaillies live in the pine forests, and divers and Slavonian grebes on hill lochs. The Flows and marshes have greenshanks and wood sandpipers, and the remote islands are the refuge of whimbrels and skuas, red-necked phalaropes, petrels and gannets.

Most of European history is connected with the influence of the monastic orders on civilisation. Hence, a visit to Iona should be part of a trip to the Highlands.

The monastery of Iona was founded in 563 by St Columba, who arrived with twelve followers. From here his monks travelled over much of Scotland, preaching Christianity to the itinerant Picts. When Columba died in 597 his influence had spread gradually throughout the glens and islands to the remotest communities, bringing the language and religion that have shaped the thoughts and lives of their descendants to this day. Hand in hand with the spiritual teaching came the traditions of those who brought it, binding the remote past to a distant future. Iona was the burial place of Scottish kings and chieftains for hundreds of years. Today, the abbey has been much restored.

The highest mountains in Scotland are the Grampians, in the central highlands, with Ben Nevis at 1,343m (4,046ft) being the highest peak in the UK. New skiing resorts are beginning to develop nearby, and may soon become as well-established as those around Aviemore in the Cairngorms. The latter is now a very popular resort with all the necessary tourism infrastructure to offer a good skiing holiday.

Wales
The people of Wales, like the Scots, have a very strong sense of national identity and a fierce pride in their country and heritage.

The word 'Britain' derives from Greek and Latin names which probably stemmed originally from the Celtic language. This is also reflected in the name of a region of north-western France, 'Brittany' in English, settled by migrants in the fifth and sixth centuries BC. Although we see from prehistoric sites, such as Stonehenge and Avebury, that there were earlier inhabitants in these isles, it was only with the arrival of these later people that Britain emerged into recorded history.

From about 600BC Celtic (Brittonic) placenames begin to appear, and the main examples of the Brittonic type of Celtic language are Welsh and Cornish. A language, as we will see, which the Welsh wish to hang onto. Some elements of the Welsh language are found in settlement names. For instance 'caer' means fortress, as in Caernarvon or 'fort in Arfin' and Caerphilly or 'Fort of Ffili'; 'aber' means river mouth, as in Abergavenny, 'mouth of the river Gafenni'; and 'tre' means farmstead, as in Trefant, 'brook farm', and Tremain, 'farm of the stones'.

With the departure of the Romans in the fifth century AD there was a considerable period of time during which much of Britain was raided by Angles, Saxons and Jutes. It is from the Angles that the word 'England' derives. During this period, however, the Britons or Celts maintained an independent existence in the areas of both Wales and Cornwall.

Even after the invasion of the Normans in 1066, Wales managed to remain a Celtic stronghold for a further two centuries, albeit within an English sphere of influence. Edward I of England was the monarch who brought Wales under English domination and placed her, for the most part, under the same laws as England. The success of his campaigns were due to a great extent to the death in battle of Prince Llewelyn of Wales in 1282. In 1301 Edward's heir was created Prince of Wales. Since that date the first son of the monarch has always had bestowed on him the title of Prince of Wales, giving the Welsh their own special relationship with royalty and the Crown. Prince Charles, the present heir to the throne, was invested with the title by the Queen at Caernarvon Castle in 1969 at the age of twenty.

Despite Edward I's victory, the spirit of independence remained and a strong upsurge led by Owain Glyndwr took place in the fifteenth century. However, with the accession to the English throne in 1485 of Henry VII, of the Welsh House of Tudor, matters settled down again. And in 1536 and 1542 the Acts of Union united England with Wales administratively, politically and legally.

At the same time as making his son the Prince of Wales, Edward I built a string of Byzantine-style fortresses right across Wales at Conwy, Caernarvon, Harlech, Beaumaris, Builth, and many more places in order to try and control the Welsh tribes whom he had conquered.

Altogether there are some two hundred castles in Wales. Many pre-date Edward I, such as the giant medieval castle

169

of Caerphilly and others which were built on sites previously occupied by motte-and-bailey castles, dating to the Norman conquest. Surviving still is the native Welsh castle at Dolwyddelan, where Llewellyn the Great is said to have been born.

Welsh heritage is also reflected in her lovely chapels, churches and cathedrals. Tintern, Neath and Valle Crucis are impressive remains of Cistercian abbeys. Still very much in use today are the splendid cathedrals of St David (Pembrokeshire), St Asaph (Clwyd), and Llandaff (Cardiff). An interesting historical background to the rich heritage of Wales is provided by her many museums, of which the best-known is at St Fagans near Cardiff, the capital of Wales.

Cardiff

Strangely enough, Wales did not have a capital city until 1956, when the present Queen officially bestowed that honour upon Cardiff, making it the youngest capital in Europe.

The history of Cardiff goes back 1,900 years, when the Romans had to fight their way against the fierce Silures into South Wales. They reached Cardiff in AD76, and built a stronghold at the point where the River Taff meets the sea. They started with a wooden structure, but as Cardiff grew in importance it became a Roman naval base with a stone fortress, parts of which still stand today.

Not much is factually known about the region during the Dark Ages, though legend tells of associations with Merlin, King Arthur and Sir Lancelot. The latter is said to have fled by sea from here.

The Normans arrived and built a primitive castle in 1093 on the site of the old Roman fort. As attacks by the Welsh tested the castle, it was strengthened and improved. When the attacks were thought to be a thing of the past, the New Hall was built against the west wall of the castle during the fifteenth century to improve the spartan living quarters. During the English Civil War sieges between the Royalists and Parliamentarians, who each controlled the estate in turn, were continuous. After the battles ceased Cardiff Castle went into decline.

Major repairs were carried out under the 3rd Marquis of Bute between 1867 and 1872, by the imaginative architect William Burges. Colourful and lavish interiors abound, and in the banqueting hall, a natural venue for medieval treats, splendid murals tell the history of this famous castle. Other magnificent improvements can be seen in the exquisite Moorish room and magnificent clock tower.

In 1947 the then Marquis of Bute presented the castle and Bute Park to the city, and today they give pleasure to inhabitants and visitors alike. Special lunches, and historic and musical banquets at the castle provide excellent entertainment for groups.

Cardiff is a beautiful city, whose Civic Centre lies in 24.3ha (60 acres) of parkland which reaches to the centre of the city, blending the grand buildings of the Welsh capital with the boulevards of Cathays Park. Sensible planning has preserved the older historical features, and the city centre with its pedestrian precinct combines modern presentation and ease of access with Victorian arcades and markets. University buskers, obviously highly talented, provide considerable musical entertainment in the pedestrian malls during the summer.

Music and drama
There is much music and drama in Wales. The Welsh National Opera is justly famous. Special festivals in Wales, called eisteddfodau, encourage Welsh literature and music. The Royal National Eisteddfod is an annual event entirely in Welsh, which has competitions in music, singing, prose and poetry.

The town of Llangollen has extended its eisteddfod to include artists from all over the world, who take part in its annual International Musical Eisteddfod. Among the great Welsh artists who have participated in this event are Dylan Thomas, Sir Geraint Evans and Dame Gwyneth Jones.

The Welsh people are determined to keep alive, and where necessary revive, their native language, which is Celtic in origin and resembles Breton, as spoken in Brittany, France. Television programmes are transmitted on a daily basis in Wales by *Sianel 4 Cymru* (Channel 4 Wales). An active local radio and press include Welsh programmes and Welsh publications. Bilingual education is encouraged in Welsh schools, and measures adopted in 1960 to revive the language include recognising the equal validity of Welsh with English in the law courts. In 1988, a Welsh Language Board was established to advise on matters

171

relating to the Welsh tongue. It is estimated that about one in five Welsh citizens now speak the language fluently.

The regions

Most visitors to Wales are attracted by the scenery. In the **south**, the Brecon Beacons National Park is a region of hills, forests and lakes, rivers and waterfalls. And the Gower Peninsula has some of the largest and finest stretches of sand in the whole of the UK. It was here that Sir Malcolm Campbell used to race his *Bluebird* car in his attempts at the World Land Speed Record. Today Rhossili Bay on the Gower Peninsula is a perfect centre for hang-gliding, as is Crickhowell in the Brecon Beacons.

Mid-Wales is a region of gently rolling hills and lush green valleys, dotted with busy market towns and villages. In this area, midway between the tiny village of Portmerion, built by the late Sir Clough Williams-Ellis to fulfil his dream of an Italianate village in Wales, and Pentre Ifan Cromlech, built around 2500BC and which remains one of the finest megalithic monuments, is the Strata Florida Abbey. This abbey, which was established in the twelfth century, stands in a beautiful setting in the hills near Tregaron. It is just one of the beautiful sites to be found in mid-Wales.

North Wales is dramatic and mountainous. Snowdonia and Cader Idris are the best-known of many peaks. The highest mountain is Snowdon, at 1,085m (3,560ft). Altogether the Snowdonia National Park covers 217,560ha (840sq miles) of unspoilt mountains, lakes, forests and coast.

Wales is a walker's paradise, and a path runs the entire length of the country from north to south. Well-marked and well-known, for 96 of its 270km (60 of its 168 miles) the footpath follows Offa's Dyke, the distinctive earthwork that was built in the eighth century as a frontier between England and Wales. King Offa, of the English middle kingdom of Mercia, is thought by many experts to have been responsible for its construction. It seems likely that it was an agreed marker to control trade and the movement of people.

Wales is also the home of many narrow-gauge railway networks upon which run a number of most attractive steam engines. Their routes range from only 1.2km to 21km (¾ of a mile to 13 miles), and most of them are privately run. Two examples are the Snowdon Mountain Railway, which opened in 1896 and climbs 914m (3,000ft) from Llanberis to the summit of Snowdon, and the 21km (13 miles) Ffestiniog Railway which runs from the harbourside at Porthmadog to Blaenau Ffestiniog. The latter is the longest and most spectacular of the preserved Welsh narrow-gauge railways. When the line first opened in 1836, horses were used to pull the empty wagons uphill, where they were loaded with slate and returned to the port by gravity. The slate was then transported by ships to all parts of the world. In 1863 the first steam locomotive was introduced. Soon after, the first of the double-ended Fairlie locomotives was used on this narrow line of only 600mm (11.5in) gauge. They have been in service ever since, except during the period of abandonment between World War II and 1954, after which the line was privately restored.

The main areas of settlement in Wales are the coastal region and the southern valleys, where 70 per cent of the population lives, and the chief urban centres are Cardiff, Swansea, Newport and Wrexham.

Northern Ireland
Northern Ireland is, at its closest point, only 21km (13 miles) from Scotland. There is a 488km (303 mile) border with the Republic of Ireland, running along the south and west sides of the Six Counties.

Around two-thirds of Northern Ireland's population are descendants of Scots and English settlers who crossed to north-eastern Ireland from the mainland of Britain back in the seventeenth century. The descendants of these settlers are mainly of the Protestant faith, have a traditional allegiance to the British Crown, and wish to maintain their union with Westminster and Great Britain. The remainder, over a third, are Irish in origin and are in the main Roman Catholic. Many of them feel allegiance with the south and favour union with the Irish Republic.

In recent years there has been considerable discontent between the two factions which has, on many occasions, been fuelled by acts of atrocity committed by extremist groups. The UK government's policy at the moment is that there will be no change in Northern Ireland's constitutional status as part of the UK without the agreement of the majority of the people of Northern Ireland. A 'border poll' in 1973 showed that a clear majority wished to remain part of the UK.

The British government continues to support the principle of a devolved form of administration, which it believes would best meet the needs of Northern Ireland, provided that it was acceptable to both factions of the community. At present a situation of deadlock persists and requires the Ulster Constabulary and a large part of the British army on duty there to maintain the status quo. At present, Northern Ireland returns seventeen members by public vote to the UK parliament.

In the centre of Northern Ireland is **Lough Neagh**, the largest freshwater lake in Ireland or Great Britain at 381sq km (147sq miles). The lake is popular with boating enthusiasts and many cruisers are rented out for weekly vacations. It is fed by numerous tributary streams from the Upper Bann, which enters from the south, and is drained northward by the Lower. Several of the tributaries are good for salmon and trout.

Of great scenic interest is another waterway in County Fermanagh, the River Erne, which winds its way through the middle of the country. It too is popular with boating enthusiasts and fishermen because it covers a wide area with the **Upper** and **Lower Lough Ernes**, both of which are strewn with small islets.

Enniskillen, the main town, stands between the two lakes. Worth a visit are the remains of the old castle, which retains part of its seventeenth-century tower and has a good set of chimes. The regimental colours of the Royal Inniskilling Fusiliers hang in the choir. The town is also made famous by the Irish ballad, 'The Enniskillen Dragoon'.

Three km (2 miles) north of Enniskillen are the fine remains of an early monastic site, founded by St Molaise in the sixth century. The most outstanding building is the Round Tower, a pencil-like structure some 26m (85ft) high. It was into this tower that the early monks would retreat during the Viking raids. This particular tower is the most perfect in all Ireland.

Belfast is the capital of Northern Ireland and is fairly modern. Its people have a reputation for being hard-headed businessmen but they also share the Irish love of good talk and music. The city developed quickly with industrialisation in the nineteenth century. Historically it has been associated with the linen industry and shipbuilding. Shipyards were first founded on the River Lagan in 1791. Since that date Belfast has built some of the largest ships in the world. The *Titanic*, which struck an iceberg on her maiden trip to New York in 1912 and was lost with 1,500 people aboard, was built at Belfast. She was the largest ship in the world at that time.

In the centre of Belfast is Donegal Square. This is dominated by the vast City Hall built in 1906. From here the busy shopping streets of Belfast fan out. Because it is a relatively modern city it has few buildings of historic interest. However, just outside Belfast, on a magnificent site on high ground, stands Stormont. It was built in 1928 of Portland stone, on a plinth of grey Irish granite quarried in the Mourne mountains, a significant choice of building materials for the construction of the buildings that were to house (however uneasily) the Northern Ireland Parliament.

To the north of the city is Cave Hill, rising to about 300m (1,000ft). It is a great natural park and, being very near the city centre, is a very popular recreation place for the people of Belfast.

South of Belfast in the county of Down are the **Mountains of Mourne**, one of the many beautiful places in Ireland about which songs have been written. Nearby is the town of **Downpatrick**, where St Patrick is reputed to have been buried.

One of the world's outstanding geological curiosities is in County Antrim – the **Giant's Causeway**. The Irish name for the phenomenon is, typically, a romantic one – the giant's stepping-stones – but the truth is more ordinary. Cooling lava split into many regular columns, mostly with six sides each, to create this wonderful spectacle.

North-west of Belfast is the historic city of Derry. St Columba founded a monastery here in AD546 and later a town grew around it. In the seventeenth century the city and surrounding area were granted to the citizens of London by King James II. The city then became known as **Londonderry** (the beautiful, traditional Irish melody known as 'The Londonderry Air' was first written down at Limavady in the county of Londonderry). Londonderry's old walls are wonderfully preserved. There are four old city gates still in existence.

13

The Channel Islands and The Isle of Man

The Channel Islands, along with the Isle of Man, have a unique relationship with Britain. Although they are not part of the UK, the British Nationality Act of 1948 declares that 'a citizen of the United Kingdom and colonies may, if on the grounds of his connection with the Channel Islands or the Isle of Man he so desires, be known as a citizen of the United Kingdom, Islands and Colonies'. Her Majesty's government is responsible for their defence, their international relations and, ultimately, their good government.

Regarding the EC, broadly speaking the Channel Islands and the Isle of Man remain outside the Community, except for customs purposes and for certain aspects of the Common Agricultural Policy. The citizens in both these territories benefit from Community provisions relating to the free movement of people and services.

The Channel Islands

These islands are a delightful enigma. Their historical ties and physical closeness to France have given their laws, customs and food a distinctly Gallic flavour. Although today they are self-governing, they owe their allegiance to the British Crown.

Their historical connection with France began when they were added to the Duchy of Normandy in AD933 by Duke William I. Another William of Normandy won a victory over the English at the Battle of Hastings 133 years later, and had himself crowned William I of England, thus uniting Normandy and England.

When King John of England lost the Duchy in 1204 to Philip of France, the Channel Islands remained loyal to the English Crown. Nevertheless the islanders like to remind the English that they were part of Normandy before being part of us, and that England was really just an extension of the domain of Normandy. Their loyal toast is always given to 'The Queen, Our Duke'.

When the Normans conquered the Channel Islands they brought with them a code of laws, called *Le Grand Coutumier*, which were excellent for the defence of human rights and which remain the basis of common law within the Bailiwicks (see below). The most unusual of the Norman legal survivals is the *Clameur de Haro*, based upon calling for justice in the name of Rollo, 'Ha-Ro', an ancestor of William the Conqueror. Any citizen feeling himself wronged by some action has only to go down on his knees and cry before the appellant and two witnesses '*Haro! Haro! Haro! À l'aide mon Prince! On me fait tort*' (Help, my prince! They are wronging me), and then repeat the Lord's Prayer in French. Instantly, whoever is committing the alleged wrong must desist until the case is tried in court.

The power of this law is best exemplified in ancient chronicles, when the cry was raised against the dead body of William the Conqueror. The story behind the event is that William, when erecting the Abbey of St Stephen at Caen, which he intended for his own sepulchre, failed to pay one man for his house site which had been requisitioned during the development. Later, when the body of William was brought to its resting place, the grave was in that part of the grounds where the house had stood. During the funeral rites the house-owner raised the Haro for justice, and it was only when the King of England's officials had paid compensation that the body could be laid to rest.

Jersey
The Channel Islands today are divided into two Bailiwicks, Jersey and Guernsey. Like one of her famous daughters, Lillie Langtry, whose warmth, beauty and personality led her to become a mistress to the former Prince of Wales and a byword in Edwardian society, Jersey – the largest Bailiwick – is most attractive. Her sunny nature has placed her first eleven times in the British Sunshine Record over the past twenty years. Summers stay long, winters are mild and spring is a blaze of flowers. The island is 14.5km (9 miles) from east to west and 8km (5 miles) from north to south, and lies only 22.5km (14 miles) from the French coast.

The west coast contains an enormously long, sandy beach known as St Ouen's Bay, which is famous for its excellent watersport facilities. The east coast is guarded by the magnificent castle of Mont Orgueil overlooking the attractive little port of Gorey, whose waterside restaurants are a byword in French cuisine.

The north coast is a domain of small bays and rugged cliffs and from here the land slopes down to the south coast, making the island a suntrap throughout the day. On the south coast lies St Helier, the capital and main shopping centre. Like all shopping centres in the Channel Islands, all goods are free of VAT as well as being duty-free, making shopping, drinking in a pub and eating out inexpensive.

Historical attractions are numerous and include two covered markets. The Central Market, opened in 1882, has thirty-seven pillars to support the roof and dome, which originally contained 81 tonnes (80 tons) of glass. Across the way is the Old Market or Fish Market. Both markets are full of stalls which are always laden with a wide variety of products. Royal Square, which was originally the town's market place, is today bordered with chestnut trees and is the spot where people are inclined to meet friends.

Fort Regent, by the capital's shoreline, was built between 1806-1814 to protect the town against possible invasion by Napoleon. This venue has now become the main leisure centre of the island. It has everything from a concert hall to roller-skating facilities, including a swimming pool, squash courts, funfair, restaurants, bars, discotheques and an aquarium.

Just off the shore is Elizabeth Castle in St Aubins Bay, which was built at the end of the sixteenth and in the early part of the seventeenth centuries to protect St Helier as it grew in commercial importance. It is built on an islet where St Helier, son of a Beligan noble, took up residence as a hermit in the sixth century. Beheaded by pirates, he is said to have picked up his head and walked away, leaving his assassins shaking with fear. The first governor of the sixteenth-century fort was Sir Walter Raleigh, who named it Fort Isabella Belissima, in honour of his queen. During the Civil War a Royalist, Sir Philip de Carteret, held Elizabeth Castle while his wife held Mont Orgueil.

The castle is reached by a causeway, which is exposed at

low tide, from the esplanade in front of the Grand Hotel. At high tide in summer the castle can be reached by amphibious craft. There is an introductory exhibition near the entrance of the castle, giving its history. Other interesting exhibits are the barracks in the Lower Ward and the interior of the Governor's House, where there are historical tableaux of famous people and events that have affected Jersey's history.

The island's history goes back long before medieval times and the visitor should see La Hougue Bie, Grouville, which was built by Neolithic man around 3000BC. The tomb has a 10m (33ft) entrance tunnel and is covered by a 12m (40ft) mound of earth, limpet shells and rubble. The tunnel leads into the main chamber, with two side chambers and another large chamber, the whole being cruciform. The central chamber may have been a place of worship with the side rooms being used for burial. The top of the mound is reached by following the circular path. There, the visitors will find two chapels. They are both now covered by the same roof but they were built centuries apart. Notre Dame de la Clarté was built in the twelfth century and the Jerusalem Chapel in the sixteenth century.

The Archaeological Museum of the Société Jersiaise has on display a replica of a magnificent Bronze Age torque or necklace which must have been worn by a chieftain 3,000 years ago. It contains 737g (26oz) of gold. The original is at the Jersey Museum in St Helier.

Among the many interesting churches on the island one in particular is uniquely attractive, and that is St Brelades on the south coast sea-shore. It has a saddle-back tower and Celtic turret. The original church was a monastic chapel which was believed to have been founded by St Brendan the Navigator when he came across from Ireland in the sixth century, searching for the Isles of the Blest. Driven by tempest to seek shelter here, he gave his name to the parish and the chapel, which was built from huge granite boulders taken from the sea-shore. Crushed shells and sand boiled in sea water were used to make the mortar, and whole limpet shells can be seen embedded in the granite.

In modern times the most famous foundation must be the Jersey Wildlife Preservation Trust, formed by Gerald Durrell in 1963. Here visitors can see over 1,200 rare and endangered species, including snow leopards, cheetahs, orang-utans, marmosets and parrots, as well as a magnificent reptile collection. The star resident is Jumbo the gorilla, who has fathered more offspring than any other of his kin in captivity.

Jersey has a reputation for its cuisine and each year the Tourism Committee holds a 'Good Food Festival'. Invited food and wine experts arrive from France and Britain to choose the winning restaurants, and a list of the various restaurants and their awards is available from the tourist board offices in London and St Helier. The island's speciality is seafood.

Guernsey

The Bailiwick of Guernsey is made up of a number of unique islands, poetically described by Victor Hugo as 'pieces of France that fell into the sea and were picked up by England'. Closest to the French mainland is **Alderney**, the place from which the arrival of the Spanish Armada was signalled to Drake and the waiting English fleet.

From the golf course on the east coast, one can look across the tidal 'Race' and, on a fine day, see the sun glinting on the windscreens of French cars driving along the Cotentin Peninsula in Normandy. A bicycle ride round the island takes 3hr and a good tip is to ride round in an anticlockwise direction, because the gradient is more downhill and less strenuous.

On the west coast the tidal 'Swinge' gargles round the rock of Burhou island, isolating it and making it a sanctuary for puffins. Bird-watchers can stay overnight for very little money in a cabin with primitive cooking facilities, provided permission is sought from the State Office in Alderney.

Alderney has as its capital St Anne, whose architecture and granite pavements remind one of a Cornish village. During the eighteenth century the town was referred to as St Anne (having previously been known as St Mary) and parochially called by the islanders 'La Ville'. On Chevalier de Beauraims's map of 1757 the map is marked as 'La Ville or St Anne'.

The lovely parish church was designed by Sir Gilbert Scott in the transitional style from Norman to Early English Cruciform, to hold a congregation of both the garrison and the islanders. All that is left of the original parish church is the clocktower which is now the oldest remaining building.

Close to it is the town school, founded in 1790 by John Le Mesurier and the inscription is recorded over what is now the Alderney Society's Museum. This houses a collection of the island's treasures, of which the most important are items from the Iron Age settlement discovered at Les Huguettes, Longy.

The north end of Alderney, between Braye and Longy Bay, is low-lying and comprises one third of the island. It is here that the beaches are safest. Around the north-east wall of Fort Albert is the symmetrical sandy beach of Saye which, along with the adjoining beaches of Arch Bay and Corblets Bay, offers the best bathing. The nineteenth-century fortresses which form an arc at the north end of the island were nearly all refortified during the German occupation.

For visitors' pleasure the Alderney Railway Society has, for the past decade, been operating a return service between Braye Road and the Quarry on the old Mineral Railway Track. Trains run every half-hour during summer weekends. This is the first and last standard-gauge railway in the Channel Islands. It started operation in July 1847.

Today there is a goodly selection of reasonably priced hotels and guesthouses, as well as restaurants providing an imaginative blend of English and French cooking.

Sark, between Alderney and Guernsey, is as beautiful as it is remote. Like an original set in a favourite play, its background has not changed in fifty years. Caught in a time-warp, there are no cars on the island, and life is lived at the pace of rural England before the Industrial Revolution. All transport is on foot, or by bicycle or horse and carriage. The ambience is that of a village community. Over the decades, only the hotels have altered, in that most rooms now have bathrooms en suite. The food remains the best of local produce, with fish fresh from the sea and cream and butter the colour of a gold sovereign from the farms.

The main disembarkation point nowadays for passenger boats arriving at Sark is Maseline Harbour on the east coast. Here, visitors who have come to stay are met and, with their luggage, driven by tractor to the top of the steep harbour hill, where they are often transferred to a horse-drawn carriage which takes them to their hotel.

Sark consists of two peninsulas. Little Sark hangs like a

pendant earring from the ear of Great Sark. A narrow isthmus – La Coupée – joins the two. The existing causeway was built by German prisoners under British military supervision at the end of the last war. In the nineteenth century tenants on both sides maintained that it was the responsibility of the other side to maintain La Coupée and children who went to school from Little Sark had to go on their hands and knees in high winds in order not to be blown 80m (260ft) into the sea below.

The island is geographically constructed like a natural fortress with cliffs rising 91m (300ft) out of the sea. At low tide the visitor will find that the cliffs are indented with fascinating caves to explore. But it must be remembered that tides run dangerously fast in this area, and it is easy to get cut off.

In Greater Sark the best sandy beaches for swimming are Derrible, with interesting caves, and next to it, Dixcart Bay which shelves gently and is the best place for children. On a clear day the outline of Jersey is visible from here. Off the west coast of Great Sark is the island of Brecqhou, on which is one of the forty private and heritable farms. The owner pays his dues to the Seigneur.

Guernsey is the main island in the Bailiwick and is itself a popular holiday venue. Considerably larger than both Alderney and Sark, its capital St Peter Port is a favourite shopping centre. Wines, spirits and tobacco are free of duty and there is no VAT to pay on luxury items.

Eating out in pubs is inexpensive and there are plenty of good standard resort hotels in Guernsey. If you like to be in the centre of things try the charming Old Government House, or the Duke of Richmond, both in St Peter Port. For haute cuisine, try La Fregate which has a wonderful menu but not many bedrooms. In the north of the island, by L'Ancresse Common and Bay, there is a golf course and many fascinating Stone Age remains. Pause by the sixth tee box to look at the Megalithic tomb of L'Autel des Landes, or at the seventeenth green to look at La Varde Dolmen. There are so many archaeological remains on this golf course that, if you are not playing to your best standard, it is possible to give up and go sightseeing instead.

The best region for swimming and surfing is the north-west coast, and beaches cover an 8km (five mile) stretch from Grand Havre Bay south to Vazon Bay.

On the north-west coast is the attractive little harbour town of St Sampson. It was here that Christianity was brought to Guernsey in the sixth century by the Welsh saints Sampson and Magloire. The twelfth-century church is built on the original sixth-century site and has an interesting saddle-back tower. In the eighteenth and nineteenth centuries granite was shipped out of here in quantity to England, and the steps of St Paul's in London were quarried in Guernsey.

The visitor will find the *Blue Guide to the Channel Islands*, published by A & C Black, the most informative book on what to see. It includes detailed information on the new museum, which has won a multitude of awards for presentation of the geographical and historical background of the Channel Islands. Castle Cornet, at the entrance to the harbour of the main town St Peter Port, tells of the continual ancient battles of the English against the French, who tried to invade the territory. For the other side of the story visit Hauteville House, where Victor Hugo made his challenging statement about the Channel Islands being 'pieces of France that fell into the sea and were picked up by England'. Victor Hugo lived for fifteen years in this amazing self-decorated and interesting panelled house, which reflects his many talents and artistic tendencies. It was in Guernsey that he wrote several of his greatest books, including *Les Misérables* and *Les Travailleurs de la Mer*.

The Isle of Man

The island, which is 53km (33 miles) long and 19km (12 miles) wide, was originally called Mona by the Romans. Later on it came under the sovereignty of Norway until it was annexed by Scotland in the thirteenth century. Subsequently it passed to the Earls of Derby for a period, before eventually coming under the direct administration of the British Crown in 1765. Today the Isle of Man has its own parliament, or Tynwald, and its own laws and taxes.

The capital of the island is Douglas, whose extensive sandy beaches and 3.2km (2 mile) promenade make it a popular venue for holidaymakers. Much of the transport seems to belong to a bygone age, as electric trams connect the town with Port St Mary and Port Erin, and even horse-drawn trams, known locally as toast racks, remain a feature of the resort.

On Prospect Hill stands the House of Keys which is home of the Tynwald or Manx parliament. Nearby the Manx National Museum introduces the visitor to much of the island's history, with its displays of folklore collections, local antiquities and natural history. One of the island's famous citizens, Sir William Hilary, founded the National Lifeboat Institution and in 1832 he erected a tower of refuge for shipwrecked mariners, which can be seen on the offshore Conister Rock. The Castle Mona Hotel was once the residence of the Duke of Atholl, the last Lord of Man.

Castletown, situated on Castletown Bay and the River Silverburn, is the ancient capital of the island. The fourteenth-century medieval Castle Rushden retains the one-handed clock presented by Elizabeth I. The *Peggy*, which is probably the oldest schooner-rigged yacht, is on display in the town's nautical museum.

Peel, which is on the west coast directly across the island from Douglas, is a pleasant resort with a sheltered harbour. St Peter's Church is a pre-Reformation building which was rebuilt in 1816. Another site worth visiting is the ruins of the cathedral on St Patrick's Isle, built in the thirteenth century and later. The mountain of Snaefell is 620m (2,034ft) high and the island's highest point. One way the summit can be reached is by a narrow-gauge railway.

Annual TT motorcycle races have brought considerable fame to the Isle of Man and the motorcycle circuit roads are closed to traffic during the races. The Tourist Trophy races take place in June and the Manx Grand Prix in September.

Ferry and air services from the mainland of Britain and Ireland provide easy access to the Isle of Man.

14
Practical Information

Keeping in Touch with Home

Obviously people who come to the UK will wish to communicate with family and friends back home, and may well wish to build this into their budget for living in the UK. To give an idea of the cost of telephoning home, and sending letters and parcels, we have set out below a series of charts in order to give you an idea of the cost of keeping in contact.

International Calls

The International Dialling Code is **010**. If you do not know the telephone number, you can get help by ringing International Directory Enquiries on **153**. If you do know the telephone number but have difficulty getting through, or if the number you want can't be dialled direct, ring the International Operator on **155**.

Charge Band A: Belgium, France, West Germany, Netherlands
Cheap Times: Mon-Fri 20.00-08.00 and Sat and Sun all day
5 min costs £1.72
Standard Times: Mon-Fri 08.00-20.00
5 min costs £2.13

Charge Band 2A: Italy, Spain, Portugal
Cheap Times: As above
5 min costs £2.02
Standard Times: As above
5 min costs £2.48

Charge Band B: Austria, Finland, Norway, Sweden
Cheap Times: As above
5 min costs £2.33
Standard Times: As above
5 min costs £2.83

Charge Band C: Canada, Jamaica, USA, Algeria
Cheap Times: As above
5 min costs £2.99

Standard Times: Mon-Fri 08.00-15.00 and 17.00-20.00
5 min costs £3.49
Peak Times: Mon-Fri 15.00-17.00
5 min costs £3.85

Charge Band D: South Africa, Guyana, Saudi Arabia, United Arab
Emirates
Cheap Times: As above
5 min costs £4.30
Standard Times: Mon-Fri 08.00–20.00
5 min costs £5.26

Charge Band E: Australia, New Zealand, Hong Kong, Singapore
Cheap Times: Every day 24.00–07.00 and 14.30–19.30
5 min costs £4.00
Standard Times: Every day 07.00-14.30 and 19.30-24.00
5 min costs £6.78

Charge Band G: India, Japan, Malaysia, Pakistan
Standard Times: At all times
5 min costs £7.08

Making a Reverse Charge Call
Visitors to the UK can make a collect (reverse charge) or
telephone credit card call home via the telephone operator in
their own country, by dialling the appropriate number from
the list below. If the caller's English is not quite fluent this
approach can help to avoid difficulties and, of course, will incur
no charges on the UK telephone bill as the call will be charged
in the caller's home country at a later date. This service is expanding to include more countries in the near future. It is called
'Home Direct'.

AT&T USA Direct	0800-89-0011
Australia Direct	0800-89-0061
Canada Direct	0800-89-0016
Directo Espana (Spain; collect only)	0800-89-0034
France Direct	0800-89-0033
Hong Kong Direct	0800-89-0852
Italia In Diretta (collect only)	0800-89-0039
Japan Direct	0800-89-0081
Korea Direct (South)	0800-89-0082

MCI Call USA	0800-89-0222
Nederland Direct	0800-89-0031
New Zealand Direct	0800-89-0064
Singapore Direct	0800-89-0065
Suoraan Suomeen	0800-89-0358
(Finland; collect only)	
Sweden Direct (collect only)	0800-89-0046

To make sure that your family and friends back home can get through to you in the UK, you need to make sure that they have the right number to dial. Suppose your number is Newcastle-upon-tyne 387 0254. The STD code for Newcastle is 091, but from abroad the '0' should not be dialled. The country code for the UK is 44. Like all country codes this does not vary, no matter where the call is coming from. Therefore your international number would be 44 91 387 0254.

For more information on local and national phone calls see chapter 4 'Budgeting, Banking, Finance and Taxation' p41.

Contact by Letter
Another important way of keeping home contact is by letter. For information on the cost of overseas postage of presents or other types of packet, both by surface and by air, you can obtain a Royal Mail International brochure called *International Letter Rates* from any UK Post Office. It also provides useful information regarding customs declarations on parcels.

Several other useful leaflets are available, also from any UK Post Office, on domestic letter rates, sending valuable items through the post, parcel rates, and packaging.

Prices given for telephone charges and postal rates were correct at the time of going to press.

Tipping
Tipping in restaurants, provided a service charge has not been included in your bill (it is advisable to check on this and ask, if in doubt, whether or not a service charge has been made), ranges from between 10 and 15 per cent, 10 per cent being usual. Taxis get the same and you should always make sure that the drivers use their meters and don't give you some dreamt-up

charge. Porters should be tipped around 50p per suitcase, and cloakroom attendants between 20p and 50p depending on the class of the establishment. The attendants in some of the more expensive hotels will leave a plate with several pound coins on it to encourage you to pay more. This is not necessary. If drinking in a hotel bar, leave approximately 10p to 30p depending on the size of your round of drinks. Do not tip in pubs unless you are a fairly frequent customer, when it is acceptable to offer a drink to the person serving. Tipping is not expected in a self-service restaurant.

Licensing Hours for Drinking

Many pubs and hotel bars are only open at certain times of the morning/afternoon, and in the evening. Until fairly recently there were strict laws throughout the UK regarding licensing hours. These have now been relaxed, but it is worth checking on opening hours before asking a friend to your local pub for a drink.

Shops

Most shops are open between 09.00 and 17.30 or 09.30 and 18.00, six days a week Monday through Saturday. In some cases there will be half-day closing, and it is worth checking whether this occurs in your area and if so, whether it is on Wednesday, Thursday or Saturday. There is usually one day a week, generally Thursday, when department stores stay open late to enable people to shop after office hours; many big supermarkets are now open until 20.00 every night.

Electricity

The power supply is 240 volts ac and plugs fit a standard socket in the UK. Plugs for razors and some hairdryers are usually two-prong, and for lamps and fires, three-prong. You can purchase international adaptors to suit your own electric razor at most international airports, or at hardware shops in the UK.

TV and Radio

There are usually two BBC television stations and two commercial stations available. Certain fitments requiring special aerials can be purchased to enable Satellite TV to be received.

There are many local radio stations throughout the UK as well as BBC Radios 1, 2, 3, 4 and 5. Radio 1 offers mainly pop music, Radio 2 middle-of-the-road easy listening, Radio 3 concentrates on classical music and drama, Radio 4 on news and current affairs programmes as well as drama, poetry and special features, and Radio 5 on sports and children's programmes.

Libraries
There are public libraries in most towns and cities throughout the UK. They all have reference sections, which are useful sources of information on all aspects of living in the UK. The libraries also maintain up-to-date information on local groups and activities in the area. These groups and activities are a useful way of meeting people as they cover a wide range of interests.

Citizens' Advice Bureaux
Your nearest bureau can be found in the local telephone book. Here you can get advice on a wide range of subjects, personal and otherwise, some of which have been mentioned specifically elsewhere in this book.

Appendices

Appendix 1
Accommodation

Acton YWCA Centre
East Acton Lane
London W3
Tel: 081 743 3285

Ashley House
YWCA
14 Endsleigh Gardens
London WC1
Tel: 071 387 3378

Barnet Overseas Students
Housing Association
Nansen Village
21 Woodside Avenue
London N12 8AQ
Tel: 081 445 8644

Christian Alliance Centre
Secker Street
London SE1 8UF
Tel: 071 633 0128

Clubland Methodist Hostel
56 Camberwell Road
London SE5 0EN

International Lutheran Student
Centre
30 Thanet Street
St Pancras
London WC1H 9QH
Tel: 071 388 4044

International Students House
229 Great Portland Street
London W1N 5HD
Tel: 071 631 3223

International Students' Housing
Society
International House
Woolwich
Brookhill Road
London SE18 6RZ
Tel: 081 854 1418/1419

Kensington YWCA
39 Ennismore Gardens
London SW7
Tel: 071 584 3060

Lee Abbey International Students
Club
57/67 Lexham Gardens
London W8 6JJ
Tel: 071 373 7242

Lillian Penson Hall
(University of London)
Talbot Square
London W2 1TT
Tel: 071 262 2081

London Friendship Centre
3 Creswick Road
London W3
Tel: 081 992 0221

Rothamsted Overseas Housing
Association Limited
Rothamsted Experimental
Station
Harpenden
Herts AL5 2JQ
Tel: 058 27 63133

Sisters of St Dorothy
International Students Hostel
99 Frognal
London NW3 6XR
Tel: 071 794 6893/8095

Student Homes Limited
78 Fortis Green
London N2 9EX
Tel: 081 883 4336

Victoria League Students Club
55 Leinster Square
London W2
Tel: 071 229 3961

William Temple House
29 Trebovir Road
London SW5 9NF
Tel: 071 373 6962

YMCA
Great Russell Street
London WC1
Tel: 01 637 1333

Zebra House
3 Marloes Road
London W8 6LQ
Tel: 071 373 2127

Appendix 2
British Rail International Offices and General Sales Agents where BritRail Passes can be obtained:

BELGIUM
British Rail International
Rue de la Montagne 52
1000 Brussels

DENMARK
British Rail International
Kobmagergade 26E
DK-1150 Copenhagen

FRANCE
British Rail International
Rue Saint Roch 55-57
F-75001 Paris

GERMANY
Neue Mainzer Strasse 22
6000 Frankfurt/Main

IRELAND
British Rail International
123 Lower Baggot Street
Dublin 2

ITALY
British Rail International
Via Pirelli 11
20124 Milano

NETHERLANDS
British Rail International
Aurora Gebouw (5e)
Stadhouderskade 2
1054 ES, Amsterdam

SWITZERLAND
British Rail International
Centralbahnplatz 9
4002 Basel

CANADA
British Rail International
94 Cumberland Street
Suite 601
Toronto M5R 1A3

USA
British Rail Travel International
  Inc
630 Third Avenue
New York 10017

British Rail International
Suite 603
800 South Hope Street
Los Angeles
California 90017-4697

British Rail International
Suite 210
Cedar Maple Plaza
2305 Cedar Springs
Dallas TX 75201

AUSTRALIA
National Australia Bank
14th Floor
Currency House
23 Hunter Street
Sydney
NSW 2000

Thomas Cook Ltd
PO Box 354
Clarence Street
Sydney NSW 2000
World Travel Headquarters Pty
  Ltd
33-35 Bligh Street
Sydney, NSW 2000

BAHRAIN
Sunshine Tours
Unitage House
Government Road
PO Box 82
Manama

BRAZIL
Oremar Representacoes
Avenida Ipirange 324
Bloco-C-1 Andar Conj.101
CEP 01046
Sau Paulo S.P.

UAE
Thomas Cook al Rostamani
(Private) Ltd
PO Box 10072, Al Maktoum Street
Deira, Dubai

GREECE
Oceanis Travel-Tourism
4 Ipitou Street
Constitution Square
10557 Athens

HONG KONG
Destination Britain
11/F OTB Building
160 Gloucester Road

JAPAN
JTB Building
6-4 Marunouchi 1 Chome
Chiyoda-Ku
Tokyo 100

KOREA
Seoul Travel Service
Suite 508
New York Building
CP0 Box 5938
Seoul

MEXICO
Viajes Crucero
Division del Norte,
No 421-1, Col del Valle 03100
Mexico D F

NEW ZEALAND
Atlantic and Pacific Travel Intl
Parnell Place
164 Parnell Road
PO Box 3839
Parnell
Auckland 1

PORTUGAL
RN Tours
Rua Do Arsenal,
124-1 Esq - Apart. 21298
1131 Lisbon

SAUDI ARABIA
Saudi Tourist and Travel Bureau
Al Johara Building
Medina Road South
PO Box 863, Jeddah 21421

SINGAPORE
Diners World Travel Pte Ltd
7500-E Beach Road, 02-201
The Plaza

SOUTH AFRICA
World Travel Agency Ltd
13th Floor, African Life Centre
Eloff Street
PO Box 4568
Johannesburg 2000

SPAIN
Ian Dornan International
Calle Del Espejo 2 bazo izd
28013 Madrid

THAILAND
DITS Travel
140 Wirelejs Road
Bangkok 10500

ZIMBABWE
Jet Tours Ltd
Harare

Appendix 3
British Tourist Authority: UK and overseas offices
(Promoting tourism to Great Britain from overseas)

ENGLAND
Thames Tower
Black's Road
Hammersmith
London W6 9EL
Tel: 081 846 9000

AUSTRALIA
4th Floor
171 Clarence Street
Sydney
N S W 2000
Tel: (02) 29-8627

BELGIUM
Rue de la Montagne
52 Bergstraat B2
1000 Brussels
Tel: 02 511 43 90

BRAZIL
Avenida Nilo Pecanha 50-Conj
2213
Edificio de Paoli
20040 Rio de Janeiro RJ
Tel: 220 1187

CANADA
94 Cumberland Street
Suite 600
Toronto
Ontario
M5R 3N3
Tel: 416 925 6326

DENMARK
Montergade 3
1116 Copenhagen K
Tel: (01) 12 07 93

FRANCE
63 Rue Pierre-Charron
75008 Paris
Tel: (1) 42 89 11 11

GERMANY & AUSTRIA
Taunusstrasse 52-60
6000 Frankfurt 1
Tel: 069 2380711

HONG KONG
Suite 903
1 Hysan Avenue
Causeway Bay
Hong Kong
Tel: 5-764 366

IRELAND
123 Lower Baggot Street
Dublin 2
Tel: (01) 614188

ITALY
Corso Vittorio Emanuele 11
No 337
00186 Rome
Tel: 654 0821/654 0464

JAPAN
246 Tokyo Club Building
3-2-6 Kasumigaseki
Chiyoda-ku
Tokyo 100
Tel: 03 581-3603

NETHERLANDS
Aurora Gebouw 5e
Stadhouderskade 2
1054 ES Amsterdam
Tel: (020) 85 50 51

NEW ZEALAND
3rd Floor
Dilworth Building
Cnr Queen & Customs Streets
Auckland 1
Tel: (09) 31446

NORWAY
Fridtjof Nansens Plass 9
0117 OSLO 1
Tel: (02) 41 18 49

SINGAPORE
24 Raffles Place
1704 Clifford Centre
Singapore 0104
Tel: 535 2966
5352967 (Ansaphone)

SPAIN
Torre de Madrid 6 of 7
Plaza de Espana 18
28008 Madrid
Tel: (91) 241 13 96

SWEDEN
Malmskillnadsg 42 1st Floor
For Mail: Box 7293
S-103 90 Stockholm
Tel: 08-21 24 44

SWITZERLAND
Limmatquai 78
CH-8001 Zurich
Tel: 01/47 42 77 or 47 42 97

USA CHICAGO
875 N, Michigan Avenue
Chicago, Illinois 60611
Tel: (312) 7870490

USA DALLAS
Cedar Maple Plaza
Suite 210
2305 Cedar Springs Road
Dallas, Texas 75201
Tel: (214) 720 4040

USA LOS ANGELES
Rom 450
350 South Figueroa Street
Los Angeles
CA 90071
Tel: (213) 628 3525

USA NEW YORK
40 West 57th Street
New York, N.Y. 10019
Tel: (212) 581-4700

OTHER NATIONAL TOURIST ORGANISATIONS

ENGLISH TOURIST BOARD
Thames Tower
Black's Road
Hammersmith
London W6 9EL
Tel: 081 846 9000

ISLE OF MAN TOURIST BOARD
13 Victoria Street
Douglas
Isle of Man
Tel: 0624 74323

NORTHERN IRELAND
  TOURIST BOARD
River House
48 High Street
Belfast BT1 2DS
Tel: 0232 235906

THE SCOTTISH TOURIST
  BOARD
23 Ravelston Terrace
Edinburgh EH4 3EU
Tel: 031 332 2433

STATES OF JERSEY TOURISM
  COMMITTEE
Weighbridge
St Helier
Jersey
Channel Islands
Tel: 0534 78000

STATES OF GUERNSEY
  TOURIST BOARD
PO Box 23
White Rock
St Peter Port
Guernsey
Channel Islands
Tel: 0481 26611

THE WELSH TOURIST BOARD
Brunel House
2 Fitzalan Road
Cardiff CF2 1UY
Tel: 0222 499909

Index

Index